Albert Inskip Dickerson

Selected Writings

Albert Inskip Dickerson

Selected Writings

Dartmouth College   Hanover, New Hampshire, 1974

Frontispiece: Albert Inskip Dickerson 1908–1972

COPYRIGHT © 1974 BY TRUSTEES OF DARTMOUTH COLLEGE

ALL RIGHTS RESERVED

LIBRARY OF CONGRESS CATALOG CARD NUMBER 74-84230

INTERNATIONAL STANDARD BOOK NUMBER 0-87451-107-0

PRINTED IN THE UNITED STATES OF AMERICA

This book may be purchased from your bookstore or ordered directly from the University Press of New England, Box 979, Hanover, New Hampshire.

Foreword

The entire adult life of Albert Inskip Dickerson, from graduation in June 1930 to his untimely death on May 18, 1972, was devoted to the service of Dartmouth College. If the starting point is September 1926, when he arrived from Chattanooga, Tennessee, as a freshman, his intimate association with the college he loved extended over a period of almost forty-six years.

The administrative positions he held were varied; in succession he was Assistant to the President and Director of the News Service, Executive Secretary of the Alumni Fund, Executive Assistant to the President, Executive Officer of the College, Director of Admissions, and Dean of Freshmen, the position he held at the time of his death. Small wonder that students, faculty, administrative colleagues, and alumni all accorded him a very special place in the Dartmouth family. His circle of friends, both within and beyond the College, was huge; and no small part of the delight in being in touch with him came from the honesty, humanity, graciousness, and urbane wit with which he dealt with others.

These qualities were especially evident in Al Dickerson's writings. Like so many others who develop skill in the handling of the English language, he got his start as editor of his high school paper. As a Dartmouth undergraduate he was associate editor of *The Dartmouth* and undergraduate editor of the *Dartmouth Alumni Magazine*. Asked to stay on, after graduation, as assistant to President Ernest Martin Hopkins, he soon took over the editorship of *The Bulletin,* then a President's Office newsletter for alumni officers and workers, and there for fourteen years he held forth in his inimitable style. A constancy of reports on the seasonal appearance and condition of a certain elm tree seen from his Parkhurst Hall window established the fame of the Bulletin Elm, which became a sort of Dickerson trademark. Whatever he wrote throughout his Dartmouth career—correspondence, office memoranda, reports, statements about admissions or freshman year, including his celebrated Parents Letters—the Dickerson touch was there: clarity and readability embellished with adroit expression and often a waggish sense of humor. Although he did not profess to be a writer, he was well known as one in spite of himself.

Importured by his friends to do some "unofficial" writing, Al Dickerson never had the spare time to oblige them, but he had promised to undertake a book after his retirement in June 1973. It was a great loss when that plan could not be fulfilled.

The Dickerson writings selected for this book differ perhaps from what he himself would have chosen (on the far-fetched assumption that he could have been persuaded to choose anything at all), but hopefully they are a representative sampling of the many thousands of words he put down on paper in such sprightly fashion and to such good effect. This book, published at the instigation of the Board of Trustees of Dartmouth College, has been assembled in affectionate memory of one of Dartmouth's sons who did his job and lived his life with the wisdom, grace, warm humanity, and sense of fun so abundantly spread before us in his own words.

Carroll W. Brewster
Katharine B. Brock
Charles E. Widmayer

Hanover, New Hampshire
June 1974

Contents

FOREWORD v

TRIBUTE TO ALBERT I. DICKERSON xi

1. THE UNDERGRADUATE 1

2. CLASS SECRETARY 23

3. THE BULLETIN 39

4. ADMISSIONS 77

5. DEAN OF FRESHMEN 117

6. THE PARENTS LETTERS 143

7. MISCELLANY 195

List of Illustrations

Albert Inskip Dickerson, 1908–1972.   *Frontispiece*

Following page

1. Andy the Tapeworm and Linda the Louse. Below: With classmate Victor Borella, 1940.   26
2. Chatting with Coach Tom Dent, 1940.   38
3. Strolling under the campus elms, 1937.   48
4. Hurricane damage, 1938.   54
5. The famous fifth-down game, 1940.   58
6. The special Convocation of January 1942.   68
7. Director of Admissions, 1946.   80
8. With President Dickey and 1951 class members, 1947. Below: With Edward T. Chamberlain, Jr., 1947.   90
9. At Moosilauke Ravine Lodge, 1948.   100
10. With Robert K. Hage and Donald W. Cameron, 1952. Below: On the Freshman Trip, 1956.   116
11. In Parkhurst Hall, 1961.   116
12. At Moosilauke Ravine Lodge, 1964.   132
13. At Moosilauke Ravine Lodge, 1968. Below: With students, 1970.   154

14. Receiving gift from President Kemeny, 1970.
    Below: With Dean Brewster, 1970.   190

15. Accepting portrait of Sidney C. Hayward, 1963.
    Below: Freshman Fathers Weekend, 1970.   204

The photographs for this book are from the collection of Adrian Bouchard, College photographer, and almost entirely were taken by him.

A.I.D.

It has been said, wisely I think, that no man ever knows another well enough to do him justice. And I am sure there are few if any among us, beyond perhaps his family—however close we were to him in work and in fun—whose memory of Al Dickerson does not fall short of doing him justice, and not the least because we have for so long taken him for granted as being one and inseparable with Dartmouth. In the most profound sense he personified the place, or at least he personified what most of us learned to love about the place. He never thought of himself, let alone spoke of himself, as standing close to the heart of the Dartmouth experience, but that is just where he stood.

And yet he wouldn't want us to get too weighty or too abstruse or even too serious about where he stood. He might even have reminded you at this point that as an undergraduate—not, I assure you, as Dean—he had *sat* on the board of the daily "D". He was not a conspicuous devotee of the woods, but was there ever a man in the College's history who got more footage out of any tree than he got out of that great elm in front of Parkhurst Hall when, as President Hopkins' assistant, he wrote regularly to all the alumni assuring them that whatever else was wrong with God's world in Hanover the Bulletin elm still stood?

And speaking of standing up, Al Dickerson taught even the trees a lesson with the way he quietly and gently and so firmly withstood the winds of disappointment and unrequited laziness that sometimes blow on a Director of Admissions and a Dean of Freshmen. On occasion he could defend himself with a brilliantly penned six-page epistle, but this talent was more often than not used to enlighten and delight parents on the ways and by-ways of their freshmen sons. He would also want me to say that he annually did his utmost to instruct freshmen on the D.O.C. trip in the varying worth of Dartmouth classes, particularly as between his Class of 1930 and the Class of 1929, mine.

With it all, this was a man to whom was entrusted the care of others and who was true to that trust in fullest measure because he was true to a self that was about as selfless, as free of vainglory and of self-righteousness, as God has permitted any man to be.

Of him, as of few others, it can be said: where he was, there was Dartmouth also. May his example abide with us.

Spoken by President Emeritus John Sloan Dickey at the memorial service held in Rollins Chapel, Dartmouth College, on May 20, 1972.

Albert Inskip Dickerson

Selected Writings

1. The Undergraduate

In his undergraduate years, Mr. Dickerson was Associate Editor of The Dartmouth, *for which he did a column called "the Gilded Shovel," and also was Undergraduate Editor of* The Dartmouth Alumni Magazine, *for which he wrote "The Undergraduate Chair," a monthly commentary on campus happenings. His Andy the Tapeworm pieces were done in the style of Don Marquis' Archy and Mehitabel.*

The Gilded Shovel

WHY WE'RE INCOGNITO

If a dumbbell *Dartmouth* heeler
   Gets your first initial wrong;
Or writes the date a week ahead
   To kid the boys along;
Or treats the facts creatively
   In English 1–2 style—
Why, just call *The Dartmouth* office up
   And ladle out your rile.

If the N.E. gets excited
   And balls the headlines up,
Leaves out official notices
   Forgets the Barrett Cup,
Neglects the blooming Women's Club
   And such momentous stuff—
Why, just call Hanover Two–One–Eight
   And fly into a huff.

If *The Dartmouth* edits seem to you
   To go from bad to worse,
And their sophomoric authors fail
   To be a Moral Force;
If the old grads are complaining of
   This flippant, flippant drivel—
Why, just telephone to Johnny and
   Lament this blasted evil.

If the weather does not suit you;
   If the Nugget shows are tuff;
If the Frailty tries to get across
   That double-timing stuff;
If your roommate has eczema;
   If the lights are on the blink—
Why, just call up Bobby Bottome and
   Create an awful stink.

Oh, it's great to be Executive
   And have Authoritee,
But nothing looks so good to me
   As anonymity,
     Tee,
       Tee,
The cagey dope, if you ask me,
Is anonymity

May 1929

DEAR SKIP

i am writing this on one
of the jacko typewriters so
if i start cracking off
in a maudlin fashion don t
blame it on me you forgot
to leave any paper in the
dartmouth typewriter and you
ought to know boss that i
can not handle that little
detail myself goodness
gracious skip it is hard
enough for even an accomplished
tapeworm like myself to work
the keys but my soul must
have expression
exclamation point

you might think boss that
i would have some resentment
about the things
you have said
about tapeworms but i
am much too big for that
as a matter of fact skip i
have seen better days in one
of my former lives it seems
to me that i was earl of

leicester the things i
could tell you boss about
old queen liz if i were only
in a reminiscent mood
exclamation point

yes i have seen better days
but let no man despise the
meek tapeworm you would be
surprised if you knew
how much hot dope the
tapeworm gets from being
continually on the inside
but i heard some people
criticize my last installment
they seemed to think it
lacked elevation at some
points so henceforth i
am not going to dwell on the
intimate details of
my professional life after
all one s art is a personal
matter anyway eh skip
interrogation point
i will tell you about
the places i ve been
and the people i ve seen
i am one of the most travelled
of tapeworms
i was in northampton
last weekend and who should
i run into but emma the
earthworm she lives in a
little dump by paradise pond
she hasn t been the places
i have been but she

has seen things skip she
has seen things semi colon
she is always claiming kin
to me i find it quite annoying
she belongs to an obscure
branch of the family which
has long been buried in
the country she is distinctly
of the soil

well if it aint andy
says she with the usual
northampton reserve
coquettishly twitching her
clitellum frankly skip i
sometimes think she is
a trifle carnal but she
claims she is only
openminded it is my opinion
that this collegiate open
mindedness has a certain
biological flavor of course
we tape worms are above that
sort of thing but that is
neither here nor there
as a matter of fact it isn t anywhere

well hello emma i reply just
to be polite it sure is romantic
out here i remark trying to
come down to her level the
moon is swell isn t it
these northampton earthworms
usually eat up that sort of stuff
skip as you may know yeh says
emma let s go down under the

crew house and have a smoke
emma is all right in her way
but she hasn t got a poetic
soul like myself

      andy
          November 1929

ODE ON A COUPLE OF URNS

Two cement urns guard Sanborn house
   Which, passing, I am prone to think
Their lines artistic as a cow's,
   Aesthetic as the kitchen sink.
      Refrain
So very impeccably decent,
   So stolid, so staunch they stand;
So many sacks of cement
   And so many bags of sand!

November 1929

Ah the tristesse of a columnist with the swette pouringe from his browe, trying to fille the goddam collum the whyle the hornes and trumpettes maken melodye with many toottes et cetera uppe staires. Heelers buzz aboot the whyle the managerre of advertysementtes with wrathe in his eyen goeth arounde desiren to know wher the helle be the copye for the adde of the shoppe for the repayren of shoon. In truthe it be harde but the collum must be fillen. I guesse this aboute doth the tricke. So longe.

      Skippe the Shovellurr

November 1929

CHEERIO! IT'S SUNDAY MORNING!

when rosy-fingered dawn beams forth
and paints the spotless snow
and all the world wakes
fresh from sleep
do do de o do do
when birds chime forth exultantly
in florida you know
and ain t life wonderful m dear
and how s your uncle joe
cheerio cheerio
it s sunday morning

when shades of gentle purplish tint
engulf those dear blue eyes
when her sprightly trilling
laughs become just
halitosic sighs
when you wonder where the devil went
last evening a sparkling wit
and you sink down in the divan s
depths and
sit and sit and sit
then
cheerio cheerio
it s sunday morning

when you look at joan through
clouds of fog
and wonder who she is
and what the hell she s doing there
and where the hell is liz
when you d rip the frat
club playboy up
for one more flash of wit
when you re sick to death of lethargy
yet can t get rid of it
then cheerio cheerio
it s sunday morning

and you know why poets have
so often called sleep golden
and why the dance was just the sport
for savages of olden
you curse the cheery drunken stags
and hate their carefree souls
yes venus has her bounties but
she also takes her tolls
nevertheless
cheerio cheerio
it s sunday morning

when they play that same old record
for the thirty seventh time
and you think you re going raving mad
with lousy song hit rhyme
when catchy little phrases hop
like rabbits through your head
too tired to shake off ennui
too tired to go to bed
then
cheerio cheerio
it s sunday morning

when the crying need for nourishment
almost brings out a tear
yet the merest thought
of breakfast makes
you shrink in craven fear
when you wonder if it s monday yet
and if not then how soon
and why does joan eat shredded wheat
and what was lorna doone
then cheerio cheerio
it s sunday morning

oh it sure is lovely when the dawn
beams on the stinking snow
and all the world is blithe and gay
do do de o do do
when all the birdies twit away
in florida so bonny
and ain t life wonderful m dear
and how s your uncle johnny
whoops
cheerio cheerio
it s sunday morning

andy

January 1930

SONG OF A FELLOW

It's great to be a Fellow with
    A scholar's liberty,
And thumb my nose at rules and things
    That don't agree with me;
And when the roomie's clock goes off
    Just snooze there leisurely—
I love this thing called Fellowship:
    It sure appeals to me.

I don't do anything that I
    Don't have an urge to do;
I go to class when I darn please;
    My worries, they are few.
And no one knows it if I spend
    A month in Wellesley.
I love this thing called Fellowship:
    It sure appeals to me.

A Lib'ral Education is
    The nuts, undoubtedly:
If he possesses intellec-
    Tual curiosity,
A Fellow can get Culture in
    Northampton easily.
I love this thing called Fellowship:
    It sure appeals to me.

April 1929

SPRING SONG

When the air is soft and dreamy
  And the balmy breezes blow,
And the sun shines forth serenely
  On the dingy, scurvy snow,
When the streets are wet and slushy
  And you walk in sprays of mud;
When the snowballs hit your window
  With that irritating thud;—
    Well,—
  It's Spring, bigod—
    Oh hell!

When your studies drive you crazy,
  And your profs all bore you stiff;
And relations with the roomie
  Are one elongated tiff,—
(What with smoking up your cigarettes,
  And drinking up your ale,
And waking you at 2 a.m.,
  And reading all your mail)—
    Well,—
  It's Spring, bigod—
    Oh hell!

When the girl friend's correspondence,
  Is that scanty, sketchy kind:
"I am so awf'ly busy, dear";

"My work is so behind";
"I bought a lovely evening wrap";
"I get so much nice mail";
"I had the cutest darling time
   Last week-end up at Yale"—
      Well,—
   It's Spring, bigod—
      And hell!

When the Nugget shows are lousy,
   And the food gets worse and worse,
And each week-end follows week-end
   With the hurry of a hearse—
And besides you pile up overcuts—
   (Those scurvy eight o'clocks!)—
So that week-ends mean a dreary chance
Of stinking like a fox;—
      Well,—
   It's Spring, bigod—
      Oh hell!

Oh, it is a cheery season
   When the balmy breezes blow;
And the sun shines forth serenely
   On the dingy, scurvy snow;
And the campus peals out joyously
   Its Springtime Griping Song,
   And everything is lousy, stinking,
   Wet, forlorn and wrong!

   Hell!

It's Spring, bigod!

   Oh, well . . . .

Skip the Shoveler

June 1929

The Undergraduate Chair

It is strange, this aspect of cloistered serenity, this atmosphere of academic dignity, which the visitor from the "outside world" sees and feels when walking under the elms of a college campus. The spirit of wise old men seems to be in the air, and a quiet veneration for learning, and that sort of cumulative soul of the college which grows as generation upon generation of its sons go out into the world taking a part of the college with them and leaving a part of themselves. All this seems quite tangible and almost inescapable to the stranger walking the green lights and shadows of campus turfs. Yet the student, following unreflectively the loose routine of his day, is altogether unconscious of it all. And if it were brought to his attention, he would probably accuse one of frequenting the cinema and reading *College Humor*. It is rather odd.

The campus normally does look quiet, dignified, unhurried, reflective. Small groups of two and three stroll the campus walks apparently going nowhere in particular. There is none of the "I-must-get-somewhere" appearance of city sidewalk throngs. There are seldom many people visible at one time. And there is little noise. Students do call to students from dormitory windows or across the street in mild bellows. But voices do not carry far and the out-of-doors is spacious. Altogether, the cloistered aspect *is* the normal impression.

The sentimental illusion (for it amounts to that) is not hard to understand. For one thing, there is a comparative absence of mass movement. There are no morning and evening "subway rushes," no "theatre crowds." As classes change in the morning, students cross the campus in streams and rivulets, reaching their high level at 12:15 when movement converges toward the Commons corner under the impulse of a virile urge for refection. Four times a day the Nugget gives up small crowds of blinking, sleepy-eyed students. And on Saturdays, knots of talking and laughing men move toward the gym to attend sundry offerings in the multiple-ring athletic circus. All these movements are far cries from the deadly earnestness of metropolitan surges.

Moreover, the impression of movement is minimized by the spaciousness of the campus, and the wide distribution of students. When crowds do gather they converge in small streams from a wide area. And, except for football games in the fall, the College never does anything all together any more.

Finally, there is the contrast of the internal life. The under-the-elms observer wonders where everybody is. With so few people in sight, one deduces that the rest are indoors somewhere, probably in dormitory or fraternity house. Wherever they are gathered excepting when under classroom restraint, one may be sure there is little serenity and less quietude. Approximately twenty-year-olds simply aren't made that way.

At this moment, if the writer were standing under the elms, he would probably be reveling in the nocturnal serenity lying over everything. But as he writes, a godawfully noisy group of students are throwing coins at a line outside his door, with a persistent telephone bell, sundry wailing vehicles, and desultory down-the-hall and up-the-stairs shouts forming the acoustic background. And every now and then someone lets off a springtime surplus of steam with a lusty scream for no reason at all. All in all, one would hardly say that a cathedral hush prevails.

Such, then, is the cloister illusion.

But perhaps it is not altogether illusory. From walking much under serene elms one might take a little serenity unto oneself. That, at least, is the sentiment of the lines about "the still North in their hearts" and "the hill winds in their veins."

The above extended preamble is merely introductory to the observation that the cloister illusion is being temporarily forestalled these afternoons by noisy eruptions of baseball all over the place. There are intramural games on the campus, and "I'll-play-for-a-minute" games in all available open places. Nowhere—not even in the cemetery—can one get away from the shouts, the cracking of bats, and the lusty thuds of balls striking mitts. Although highly unacademic and un-serene, the campus presents a very healthy picture. One wonders about the effete and sophisticated college generation which is so copiously worried about in the magazines. . . .

While the elm trees blossom forth in their springtime charm—as the newspaper poets would say—even so doth the undergraduate. The sartorial sloppiness encouraged by the slush era is disappearing as flannels supplant the corduroys and Campion curiosities in pastel shades take the place of the green sweaters. Blazers reappear and black-and-white shoes add flashy touches. The place begins to look almost respectable.

And all the gasoline buggies. Gone (almost) is the "collegiate" Ford. The typical undergraduate vehicle is a rather neat job in the medium-priced class, usually a roadster-with-rumble. There is a growing number of cars of the kind which one turns around to look at.

The drinking problem is always brought to attention in the spring, as in the fall. It is hard to say just how much springtime restlessness actually adds to the drinking and how much normal drinking is merely made more obvious when the cheery collegian is enticed into the open by clement weather. At any rate, it is a minority proposition, and there are no "alarming trends" (borrowing from the magazine alarmists) to be observed.

Nothing has stirred "the boys" this month, excepting the house party flurry. May is a month of *laissez-faire*. One does a respectable amount of worrying, and gradually screws up courage for June. The seniors started plugging a little earlier and more vehemently with the comprehensive exams imminent at the close of the month. They expressed feelings somewhat of the nature of those experienced by whatever-battalion-it-was which first ran into a gas attack without knowing what it was.

June 1929

Hurray for Football

Football, although so frequently worried about as a menace, is one of the most cohesive factors in college life. After the football season, the College never gets all together in one place. The Webster Hall offerings, basketball, hockey—these draw but a fraction of the student body. But football somehow seems to draw all interests, even those of our more aloof scholars, and of our most rabid anti-crowd minded individuals. When the pedantic prof (a disappearing specimen) finds it necessary temporarily to seek common ground with his students, he inevitably falls on football. It seems one of the most universal autumn interests, even outside of the college world.

The Carnegie flurry over the over-emphasis and commercialization of football scarcely made a ripple in Hanover. Perhaps it was because Dartmouth seems to have a sure antidote for over-emphasis, in the Yale game. And Dr. Eli's boys apparently take a peculiar paternal interest in administering it annually. It is rather odd the way the success of the football season in the eyes of the College seems to hinge on the Yale game. After the Yale defeat, a victory is just a victory, never a triumph; and a defeat is merely a defeat, instead of a major cataclysm. We beat Brown and Cornell, and nobody shouted hallelujah; we got licked by Navy, and nary a tear was shed.

The Commercialization Evil passed into the hands of the undergraduate humorist—who is always hungry for the serious reports of serious old men—so that now one can hardly scintillate in ping-pong without finding oneself under suspicion. "Commercialized athlete!"

January 1930

The Gold-Rolled Spade

Skip the Shoveller is a personage who has forced himself on campus attention by breaking fitfully into print in *The Dartmouth* during recent months, as the author of an anomalous column called "The Gilded Shovel." He has maintained a certain imperfect but adequate anonymity. A little research on the writer's part revealed the interesting if slightly incompatible facts that Skip is a "fat boy who lives over in Hitch and drinks all the time" and a "big tall guy, slightly cock-eyed." If either of these is true, we know someone who is being called lots of names for someone else's aberrations.

Skip went amateurishly about filling what has been felt as a need of *The Dartmouth* for some time. He could hardly be called a pseudo-humorist, because he has never actually claimed to be funny. His one avowed aim is to be a Moral Force. The creed of the column is: "Nobody admires a tapeworm," a proposition which has been expounded and defended with some warmth. The ensuing controversy has brought forth a series of communications from Andy the Tapeworm, who has adopted the medium of Archy, the Free-Verse Cockroach of Don Marquis, for expressing his soul.

The Carnegie Foundation report on the commercialization of athletes brought forth in "The Gilded Shovel" an inside story on the Big Green gridiron wage slaves, which W. O. McGeehan, astute columnist of the *New York Herald-Tribune*, reprinted, apologizing for it by labelling it "Some Unseemly Levity." The most recent crusade of "The Gilded Shovel" has been against the pigeon menace at Webster Hall.

The Shoveller's "public" has watched him through an experimental novitiate in which he has tried out various ways of filling columns. When he hears only a few people say it is lousy, he figures that it is pretty good. When the loudly articulate nays are more numerous, he tries something else. He has apparently discovered that personalities are generally to be eschewed and that the border-line of smut is dangerous and usually unfruitful. When he finally gets a fairly adequate idea of what this columning business is all about, he will probably graduate, and his "public" will have to watch a new Shoveller stumble through his apprenticeship. Thus will "The Gilded Shovel" be another victim of that tragedy of undergraduate activities, discontinuity.

But tut-tut, we grow gloomy. Let us be off to cultivate our garden.

February 1930

2. Class Secretary

For ten years immediately after graduation—1930–1940—Mr. Dickerson served as class secretary for 1930 and wrote the monthly class column in the Alumni Magazine. *In his column for October 1939, printed here, he opened his tenth year with cheerful anticipation of the end of his secretaryship and revived Andy the Tapeworm, which would seem to have been the worst possible way to persuade his classmates to let him go.*

1930

Secretary-Chairman, Albert I. Dickerson
Administration Bldg., Hanover, N.H.

With mingled, i.e. blended, spirits (7 percent Olde Scribe and 93 percent neutral spirits) we approach this first stanza of the tenth and final canto. Only eight more 10th-of-the-month deadlines to meet with fact, fancy—and verbiage! Yet with this merry prospect, the tender melancholy of the end to a position of honor and malediction in a noble and ornery class—an end to being Minister of Propaganda, Public Enlightenment, Culture, and the Multiplication of the Species, repository of the pardonable pride of Thirtymen in new brides and new brats, new jobs and jocularity; Keeper of the Books, Forgetter of the Facts, and Scribbler of the Scribbles. There is a minuscule tear in our large and 99 percent delighted eye.

REFLECTIONS ON THE THIRD TERM

Unlike some others who also enjoy toasting their larynx before firesides, we take an unequivocal stand on the mooted third term question. A Yellow House spokesman (come up and see us sometime) has let it be known that we are agin' it. [A private Gallup poll (Copyright 1939) has indicated we might as well beat you to the draw.]

We are not going to be coy about this. Following this early resignation, we anticipate a surge of "Draft-Dickerson-for-1940" movements. To the "We-Need-Dickerson" clubs of Indiana, South Dakota, and the Insular Possessions, of Stamford, Chattanooga, Atlanta, and Alcatraz, greetings.

And then, at the eleventh hour, from our Norwich, Vermont, homestead, we will scribble, by lamplight, on an old piece of Kleenex, the momentous words: "We do not choose to run in 1940," and the news will go thundering down the valley, to every hamlet and hotspot, wreaking we know not what havoc and hoop-la. And that will be that.

While, realist that we are, the poll had something to do with this, the following communication, recently received, clinched it:

dear skip
you will remember me
you d better
i am andy
ten years ago i used to wrap
myself around the space bar of an old
rattletrap typewriter in the jacko
office and punch out prose and poesy with
my muscular but cultured scolex
which you published in a column
otherwise mediocre or worse
and i must say that the benefit
of my worms eye perspective on life
broadened your horizon no little skip
no little

i finally found that old typewriter
which the jacko stole from the dartmouth
way back when cowley was editor
it has since been filched by the d o c
le cercle francais il popolo romano
the council on student organizations
germania and palaeopitus and where do you
think it is now question mark
in the chess club exclamation point
and to think of the lilting prose
and free verse i have written on

1. Drawing of *Andy the Tapeworm and Lorinda the Louse* presented to Class Secretary Al Dickerson by his 1930 classmates. Below: Dickerson with classmate Victor Borella at 1930's tenth reunion.

that old wreck and now it is used
to make chess dates with harvard and
probably even bennington period
sic transit gloria wormi

well a dizzy decade has passed
debacle depression deflation
democrats debts and now
decimation

i tell you skip life
has been no bed of predigested pap
for us parasites
in and out in and out
but as prexy once said quote
change is opportunity unquote
and that goes for worms too
i have been in some pretty swell
places since 1930 and seen some
glorious peristaltic action
maybe i will tell you something
about it in my next if somebody
will leave some paper in the
typewriter

in these parlous times hanover
looks pretty nice pretty nice
through half a dozen american wars
and god knows how many others
and still a serene place for
dartmouth men and worms to come
back to i am going to be at
that reunion in june no matter
what so you might as well make
me an honorary member and invite
me otherwise the party may be
on you

I figure it is about time for a
new deal in 1930 boss
you have been an average to fair
secretary but we are due for
a change boss a change you know
perfectly well every class needs
some new blood or it goes to seed
and frankly skip 30 is getting just
a touch seedy boss a touch seedy
after all ten years is quite a stretch
i get around you know i get around
and a lot of the boys are getting
just a little bit fed and in some
spots even nauseated
at the parasites friendly society the
other night lorinda the louse who is
a lulu with a special liking for
thirtymen says andy says she
i am going to support haffenreffer
for secretary on the theory he will
throw hops to the populace
all dickerson throws is words
well i says how do you know he ll
resign he won t have to says she
but he will he will say you can t
fire me exclamation point i resign
of course he will resign i rejoins
just as a matter of form and then
a couple of dopes will tell him
what a great guy he is and he will
think it is the voice of the people
after a couple of beers they will say
skip old boy you re a great guy and
we don t want any secretary but you
and he will say tut tut eating it
up and they will say nobody but you

skip old boy and he will say well
fellows if that s the way you feel
about it you know that line lorinda
as lorinda says sometimes i think
a college education is wasted on
ninety percent of these fellows
who know they need a change but
will sit back like a lot of
gentlemanly sheep and let a time
server who fancies himself stay in
office until his too long deferred
demise if he wants to just because
they are so pusillanimously polite
well boss don t fall for it thats
all i ve got to say you have been
to sunday school and you know what
mene mene tekel upharsin means
period

well i m getting toward the bottom
of this sheet but in case you don t
think i get around i will tell you
some things about yourself snub and
mary poehler came in to see you
and broke the news which you ought
to have known if you were any kind
of a secretary namely that win hatch
your hanover neighbor is going to
pullman washington to teach biology
at the university of washington
kirk jackson popped in breathless
from golf and said he would pop
in again but didn t
al allyn the associate actuary
who usually eschews the scurrilous
scribe cautiously called at the very

end of a three weeks vacation with
daughters age six and two and got
sympathy for his sufferings from
phlebitis parenthesis more
generally known as milk leg an
affliction of nursing mothers
parenthesis closed

red alcorn the tom dewey of
the nutmeg state relaxed from
rigors of righteous prosecution
at the wizard of oz at the nugget
after sending the wicked witch of
waterbury to jail with all her
wicked winged monkeys and now
with the nutmeg legislature also
in recess red returns to peaceful
prosecution as assistant states
attorney he says paul duback got
a law degree which is not on your book
and red thinks he is practicing
in madison wisconsin it seems to
me skip you ought to know those
things question mark
phred chase the phlorida photographer
came to see you as did van and doris
vanderbeck and ed benoist after
swearing he wouldn t come anywhere
near left a note under your door
the gene zagats of various realty
corps were encountered at the
wigwam and the less said about
the joint visit of c rauch and
j chandler the better you cut a
ridiculous figure at deck tennis
with ev and dot low and their

three charming lads at lake morey
sam allen should have known better
than to ask a guy like you with
all except seat muscles atrophied
to climb the white mountains with
him but then he is used to the keen
young high school graduates with
whom he does vocational work for
the n y a in steubenville ohio

the haffenreffers and bud frenches
and the rest of the getchell gals
would rather not couple their names
with yours in print re your descent
on rhode island so we will skip
that for that matter so probably
would the john frenches who came
to hanover from woodstock to trim
the ruddy hair of their roistering
young bucks before going to
burlington vermont to practice law
fulfilling a long yearning for the
country and a non yearning for
new york for which you can t
blame them period

this is enough my delicate scolex
is worn to a nubbin pounding this
tripe you dish out so all too
copiously i was born to higher
things now take my advice to heart
and if you want some more leave
some paper in the typewriter in
the chess club love and kisses

      andy

September 1939

Vox Populi

Within a month of writing the preceding class column for the *Alumni Magazine*, Mr. Dickerson repeated his Andy the Tapeworm style for two letters to *The Dartmouth*, only this time he introduced a new character, Marmaduke the Mouse. The letters appeared in the issues of October 6 and 7, 1939.

dear mr editor
my name is marmaduke and i am a mouse
who enjoys a more or less abundant
life among the old paste jars warmed
over morsels and stale pretzel crumbs
in the jacko office they have a typewriter
here but i don t know why because
they seem to get along very well with an
old pair of scissors and a gallon jug
of mucilage they never have anything
in the typewriter except a slightly
smeared piece of blank yellow paper
but that makes it nice for me because
every night i give expression to a
really beautiful if unrecognized soul
on the blank paper and every morning
the janitor tears it out and throws it
away the fate alas of most of the
finer things archie the immortal
cockroach of don marquis gave us
poets of the so called lower forms of

life quite an idea and if only
janitors had a more alert eye for the
beautiful and profound the world would
be richer by a library of rodent and insect
literature which would make shakespeare
seem a merely facile scribbler of light
verse and most college editorials the
laments of lads bored by the curriculum
of the fifth grade but that is neither
here nor there period

mechanically i am more adept than archie
squatting lightly on the space bar with
the agile use of my forelegs i can type
faster than most of your heelers and
be a damn sight more decent to the queens
english

well yesterday hiding in the wastebasket
among mutilated copies of sundry so called
college comics i heard one of the jacko
boys laboring on the typewriter i thought
he must be writing to the editor of the
siwash smack for an exchange copy to clip
from but no semi colon he was writing
to the most sprightly and widely read
department of your paper the official
notices and i see the results in your
paper this morning to wit quote
jacko lit colon beer and idea party
in one o one hitchcock for all lit men
at eight thirty unquote
now after all boss isn t that going a
little far question mark
beer and idea party exclamation point
my only reaction to that is as follows
quote oh skittles unquote and i know

dorothy parker would feel the same way
night after night just for the love of
creating something beautiful i write
deathless prose and emancipated verse
which is baled up and sold as old paper
and these jacko boys have to sit around
in hitchcock bandying old saws
and dark brown gobbets and swizzling
beer until they can laugh at each
others gags well all i can say boss is
that the tanzis ought to get rich on
that program and why anybody should pay
twenty five cents for those same gags
on slick paper is more than i can see
anyway i don t see why they don t have
their laughing jags here in the office so
i can have the dregs after they go home

just think how easy it would be to run
this thing into the ground boss
in the same column the canoe club announces
a cider and doughnut and canoeing party
you will be getting such notices as
quote the a s u will hold a vodka
and boring from within party in the
vault of the dartmouth national bank
unquote and quote the administration
committee will hold a pluto water and
expulsion party in the gents room of
parkhurst hall unquote and then where
will you be question mark

you say vox populi have to be
signed so here is my signature
hoping for better things

marmaduke

dear boss
it was mighty white of you to print
my little piece in the paper this
a m and in boldface type too
sometimes these things look pretty
smart alecky in type don t they and
maybe it would have been a good thing
if the janitor had thrown it away too
anyway the jacko boys were burned up and
they threw the old typewriter out of
the window in a fit of petulance so
if you miss any of your typewriters
some morning you will know that the
jacko boys are writing another official
notice

i m glad you left this piece of paper
towel in your typewriter which is not
too bad except the space bar is so
jittery that it goes down if i take
a deep breath and makes a lot of extra
s p a c es   l i k e   t h i s
but w i th a little selfcontrol i get
along

theres a cheery little piece named tootsie
the termite in cozy quarters down in the
northwest leg of your desk who is
chattering as i write like mehitabel
the cat she claims a colorful string
of former existences so i put her in
her place with an unexpurgated account
of a few of my former lives because
you know boss the fact is that i ve been a
good many things in my time in
fact i have transmigrated quite freely

I began reminiscing about when i was
editor of the luxor daily isis and
osiris back in the time of one or the
other of the pharaohs the isis was
the spring edition and osiris was
the fall edition and that daily
stuff was just a touch of journalistic
license you know what that is
so we used to have a pretty good deal
of time to give matters some thought
between editions after all one doesn t
get out a handwritten edition on papyrus
or even on clay without giving it a
second thought which is perhaps just
as well in those days the curriculum
was pretty sketchy with no social sciences
whatever a slight touch of geography
only the most rudimentary notions of
chemistry and physics just some
math and astronomy and a good dose
of religion that gave us lots of
time to work on the paper and rib
old rameses and boy did we have fun
up to the time we suggested he stop
flubbing around with affairs of state
and do something really constructive
like building a pyramid which would
be very useful for him to be buried in
that was when i stopped being an editor
and turned in to an amoeba which tootsie
remarked was a darned sight more useful
an existence what do you think

well boss i was disappointed in your
boner edit i like your stuff generally
boss and with the possible exception

of some of my better pieces which the
janitor threw away i think you are easily
doing the best stuff in the building
if these activities are so artificial
why do you guys work your fool heads
off around here it s getting so bad that
there s hardly time after you go
home for me to get a decent piece done
before the janitor comes the jacko office
isn t like that to say that a
list of subfreshman activities amount to
a draft just doesn t make sense you know a
freshman isn t going to do anything he
doesn t want to maybe it is a dirty trick
to summon freshmen summarily to appear
but i wouldn t worry about it when half
the time they don t even answer official
twenty four hour notices frankly boss i
think you overstated your case to the
point where it was just silly and even if
you did have a case do you need to be so
truculent about it question mark

and you may not believe it boss but some
freshmen are actually shy tootsie says
that is so and she has seen timid freshmen
who would like to go out for your paper
chew their fingernails at your office
door and run when the door opened
because they think a college paper is
such hot stuff well i don t want to
quarrel with my boss all i ve got to
say is that if this is the hottest boner
of the year then the boys up in the ad
building stumbled along a good deal
better than the dartmouth has ever

given them credit for even in its most
complimentary sic phases and you are
going to be pretty hard up for the rest
of the year as a casus belli i think you
have something there like liberating
poland from the poles

no hard feelings i hope boss and
tootsie hopes so to

           marmaduke the mouse

2. Al Dickerson, executive assistant to President Hopkins, chatting with Coach Tom Dent at soccer practice in the fall of 1940.

3. The Bulletin

The Bulletin, *an informal newsletter reporting on College events and developments, was originally distributed only to the Alumni Council, class and club officers, and other alumni workers. Mr. Dickerson wrote it for fourteen years, 1933 to 1947, while serving first as Executive Assistant to the President and then as Executive Officer of the College.*

The fun in writing a *Bulletin* is the thought that almost any of you on the receiving end—whether you are Red Newell '24 in Shanghai or George Hall '18 in Paris or Jim Hodson '29 in Seattle or Jack Conners '14 in Bridgeport—would like at this moment to be in our third-floor, *Bulletin*-writing cubbyhole hearing a cheery wind sing as it comes down from the mountains and watching it bend the elm tops in front of this window. The warm sun makes the few persistently clinging leaves look not withered but golden. One by one they surrender their hold on the whipping branches and sail off for a last wild ride down the sky. The sky is bright blue and white through the restless elm tops. If you were here to look through this lively movement of graceful skeletons of trees, your thin horizon between window-ledge and sky would be one dominated by rooftops, familiar Hanover spires and crests of hills. On your left the warm red brick and gleaming white of the library tower against robin's egg blue; then the sharp white tip and weathervane of the White Church spire; just the peaked green cap of the hidden Bartlett tower, flanked by two tall solitary pines, the lofty skeletons of the thin, twin radio towers; the enormous, north-pointing orange arrow along the long, thin, gently-sloping, black roof-line of Webster Hall; only the apex of the pyramidal, red-tiled bell tower of Rollins Chapel; finally the shining white cupola of Dartmouth against the mottled pine-green and umber of Balch Hill's crest and the familiar Dartmouth weathervane against the sky; and at the very edge of the window frame which ends this brief, lovely stretch of horizon, a bright climactic touch—the briskly waving red and white stripes of the flag, brilliant and alive.

All this is a pretty stiff dose of freshman-theme adjectives and pathetic fallacies. But another good thing about writing a *Bulletin* is the knowledge that when one wraps verbs and adjectives around Hanover names, things and places, they will be read with the eye of affection for familiar and well loved things and not of criticism for turgid prose.

When this reaches you at the end of the week, the horizon will be the same—although the colors and "stage-lighting" may be different—but on the level below this watchtower window, the present busy activity with noisy play going on over the campus, brisk walkers on the paths, parked cars lining the streets and movement everywhere, will be replaced by silence and emptiness. Teeming activity will reach a peak at noon on Friday and a long line of overladen cars will begin to stretch over the hills toward Lebanon and on down to Boston. And external Hanover will by afternoon take on that deserted village aspect into which it lapses abruptly, as at a signal, at the half-dozen times during the year when the great exoduses take place.

Remember the excitement of the first peerade? Probably the movement has changed somewhat as automobiles have to some extent replaced the exuberant special trains; but we should guess the change is not essential. The advance planning and arranging—getting a place to stay; contracting for dates, blind, cloudy or well tried; the establishment of various complicated rendezvous, etc., etc.—all are doubtless much the same as when you did it yourself the first time. The Band playing "Dartmouth's in Town Again" in a foreign setting, expressing the solidarity of a vigorous mass invasion. And finally the hectic rushing, pushing, shoving and horn-tooting of getting to the Stadium. And finally the game itself. . . .

October 26, 1938

The campus glistening white, lushly cushioned with snow; a boy with a hockey stick; a young mother towing two little snowsuited figures on a sled, one red, one blue, over the mid-campus spot where Carnival statuary will one of these days stand; the buildings of the Row snow-white, too, and above them, to set them off, a slate sky, blue-grey, with something of the robin's egg in it, something of the pigeon's wing, something of woodsmoke hanging blue on the still grey air of winter dusk; against the buildings, the architecture of the wintry elms, and what more beautiful than the bare elms, sweeping upward and outward in strong curves and striking angles, rugged strength into delicacy and grace? Suddenly the black swirl of the Connecticut is white, immobilized in ice, dusted with snow, only a wayward streak of black water left to zigzag down mid-river, fragile-edged.

The ski tow is running. There is ice in the hockey rink. Chief Hallisey has published his annual warning not to park cars overnight in Hanover streets, impeding the hypothetical snowplow called out by the hypothetical storm. The skiers, varsity and freshmen, are riding their steel edges at breakneck pace down the slopes after wistful Indian Summer weeks of cross-country running, gymnasium exercises. The catalogues are out. Storm doors are going up. And in the post-holiday lull, the College catches its breath this week before the busy fortnight which always precedes the Christmas recess, a fortnight full of exams, course papers, arrears to be caught up, lectures and public events of all sorts, opening of the winter sports schedules, plays, Christmas parties.

Of course, snow is not news on the eastern seaboard, with radio announcers complaining of blizzards on Carolina gridirons, and snow to be shoveled off sidewalks by a large proportion of the *Bulletin's* readers. Suffice it to say that he who called the September 21 blow a "breeze" is the man who reported that Hanover had a "White Thanksgiving." How white and how *cold*!

December 2, 1938

A mild and melancholy rain falls, around the clock, yesterday, today, tomorrow, forever? Sidewalks are a peril of miniscule islands of ice in miniature lakes and not so miniature seas of water. The glory that was Eleazar, the towering figure that dominated the Carnival campus, posturing raucously by day, dwarfing in its floodlit whiteness the illuminated Baker Tower at night, is an amorphous mass of dirty slush around the blasted fragments of a dingy snow pedestal amid oceans of midcampus wetness. The list of three-score men bid to senior societies last week vied for front-page space with a Dick's House list of sniffling invalids of almost equal length. What is left of the winter's happy richness of snow is just a problem for the steam boiler which is towed about the campus to bore neat round holes in accumulations of ice and snow on top of the street drains. The misty moisture of March is everywhere, splashing up from below, dripping down from above.

But March is nice. It is one of the great solidarity builders of this closely knit community. Dartmouth men, whose nostalgic devotion to Hanover's other eleven months is one of the great sources of the College's strength, are wont to apologize for Hanover's March. Nothing, however, draws people together like adversity, the sages say. And those who pause perilously at the water's edge to greet each other these mornings with a sympathetic sniffle, pass the "timb ub day" with consonants muffled in the clogged plumbing of their crania, and mumble the words about weather which are on everybody's lips, enjoy a oneness of feeling, we propose, which is not exceeded in unity by the roaring groundswell of emotion in the Dartmouth stands after a touchdown against Yale.

And March is busy. Such has been the fulness of life in Hanover since our last that your correspondent, having been swept up in it at various points, hasn't had time to observe; and such is the pace of the march of events (we never pun consciously) that one is hard put to it to catch up, let alone get far enough ahead to pause and record.

March 9, 1939

Lines in Praise of the Bulletin Elm

I fear that you shall never see
A Bulletin without a Tree:

A Tree whose aspect from the west
Has often filled this space—when pressed.

A Tree which, looked at from the east,
Will make ten sentences, at least;

A Tree that on demand may wear
Stuff for a paragraph, or pair:

A Tree which sweeps the landscape o'er
With words for half a page or more;

A Tree that looks at me all day
And often tells me what to say.

The tree is often praised by sages:
She very neatly fills out pages.

The Bulletin is wrote by me—
Dear God, I thank Thee for the Tree!*

*Poetic praise of the Bulletin Elm elicited this response from one reader:
Dear A.I.D.: It seems to me
That you should stick to prose. Aussi
I think you're wasting College vellum
To eulogize one measly elum.

Issue Number 13—hardly the medium for wishing you a Happy New Year!

The Tree drips water and the rain bids fair to controvert the normal trend of events by giving us a Brown New Year after a White Thanksgiving.

Just ahead of the Christmas bills, comes news that the Army, agreeing with Dartmouth that the Big Green has the best coaching staff in the country, has conscripted the staff, lock, stock and barrel.

Hanover is quiet. The paths are empty. From The Bulletin Watchtower the barely perceptible lines of the dark green shutters are all that can be seen of Dartmouth Row through the thick white mist. At night the broad, massive circle of College buildings from which this village radiates are dark and ponderous. Only beacon in the evening darkness is the warm and rosy gleam of lights in North Mass, where are gathered the few students who, from remoteness of home or arrears of study, have stayed to titillate their good intentions in the enervating ease and quietude of Hanover-in-recess.

In Parkhurst Hall, administrative officers peck away at the accumulations on the corners of their desks, casting an occasional envious thought at their faculty colleagues enjoying the holiday ease, which the latter, of course, deny with accounts of unremitting industry reading papers, preparing courses.

In the prevailing silences, eyes are cast backwards on a year of big and sometimes horrifying events, of aroused spirits and thinking stirred; and forward to 1941 with speculations in which perforce there must be less of complacency, more of courage than at the threshold of many a New Year.

And so we greet you for 1941 with a warm hope if not a light word; a warm hope for the enjoyment of the good things that give satisfaction and happiness. . . .

December 30, 1940

3. Bulletin editor Dickerson strolling under the campus elms in 1937.

Maybe it is time to start in again on the Bulletin Elm. We've just been looking over the reports of Messrs. Richardson, Childs and Scarlett, and find that as we hoped (and feared) they not only have mined some rich ore from under the deeply snow-covered surface of the Hanover scene, but have also drained off the top skim of spot news which is our usual merchandise, to the last drop. Professor Richardson has popularized the academic dichotomy of Teacher and Educator, and our mail has been full of leering salutations, "Dear Educator." Our desk has groaned under the weight of this fan mail. And Professor Childs has even introduced a new tree—an alleged birch, pregnant with inspiration—surely an upstart, if not purely fictional, stripling. It certainly was not there when Tommy Longnecker and your correspondent used to look out of that window. No brilliant flashes of creative imagination leaped out from that empty area of Hanover sky in explanation of the dilatory progress of that sparkling, definitive and slightly overdue paper on Lord Byron.

Indeed, during that balmy and lotus-laden spring, when Schickelgruber was a comic little vegetable-eater and when at any distance from Wall Street the spreading quagmire of the Depression appeared a mudpuddle due soon to evaporate in the summer sun, we often had to go as far afield as Northampton, where some first-class elms grow around a body of water known to generations of Dartmouth men, and with some justice, as Paradise. Smith girls and their friends had to go there to do their smoking, in those days, and many a Dartmouth lad who never touched a butt all week had frequent seizures, on week-ends, of an irresistible craving for the weed. Paradise Pond was the ineluctable environment for the productive study of our interesting poet. Incredulous as Professor C. may have been (and may still be) there was at least one golden Sabbath in May when we spent an afternoon under one of the elms of Paradise in reasonably continuous perusal of a germane opus by one Maurois. It was only the time consumed on the way to Northampton and back that slowed our scholarship. But may the time come soon again when seniors graduate in June and when their Mays are full of that happy valedictory blend of lofty aspirations and indolent endeavor, on the threshold of bigger and better things.

Now that the *Bulletin's* public has been expanded by the forwarding plan, the Elm undoubtedly needs an introduction to its new friends. It is a tree. It is a magnificent tree that rises to a great and spreading height beside Parkhurst Hall. It is full of wisdom and of charm, and, in proper season, of leaves. The latter, to faithful readers of *The Bulletin*, are known by name, leaf-by-leaf. It is also a prolific source of words, as need arises. Last winter there was a chipper grey squirrrel named Ralph who used to jump around it, nibbling buds. Either Ralph has gone to the wars, or taken on the protective coloring of navy blue and blended into his environment. Right now three feet of the Elm's trunk are under snow. . . .

February 3, 1943

... Concerning nature-writing, we aren't going to keep harping on those 43rd Street Thoreaus, [of the *New York Times*] but we've got to make an apologetic confession of a low temptation to pun on the pathetic fallacy. It involved the Freudian conception of skyscrapers as phallic symbols, and the addition of these upper-story chickadee-fancying journalists to crediting nature with human emotions and chrysanthemums with warm feet. But the shape of the New York Times Building doesn't lend itself to this conceit, a shallow sally anyway. We dropped the whole thing. ... Furthermore, in justice, we've got to admit we liked one of their editorials last week, on Black Kettles, and have been wondering whether we ought to write a Letter to the Editor about it. Even though black kettles under some conditions have warmer feet than chrysanthemums, nothing was said about this; and none of the tenderly remembered kettles had welcoming arms or recumbent seats, like the cherished wheelbarrow.

The kettle which *we* remember most affectionately from our youth was one that the clothes used to boil in on Monday, if it didn't rain. It was attended by a wonderful woman named Allie, of the color of a horse-chestnut, of no discernible shape whatever, and blessed with a serenity invulnerable even to the highly developed malice of age ten. Unimpeded by a generous installment of snuff under her ample lip, she sang wordless improvisations all the livelong day, without interruption save to expectorate flawlessly into the embers with the legendary accuracy of a pigmy dart-blower, the sharp crack of a rifle, and about the same short-range trajectory. This was one of our earliest lessons in perfectionism. Allie was also exemplary in faithfulness and regularity, and if she missed a sunny Monday once in a while, she would explain on Tuesday or Wednesday that it was because she had contributed another dusky citizen to that merry but underprivileged community which the river faithfully flooded every spring. (Probably the TVA orders things better these days.) The arrival of these offsprings always seemed to be as much a surprise to Allie as to us—mild in both cases. Her contours never varied. And if once or twice in all those years word got through by messenger that a Monday non-appearance was attributable only to the perverseness of the jedge and the substantiality of the jailhouse, you couldn't blame Allie for the unpredictable nature of Saturday night or the deplorable qualities of gin and husbands. . . . Another beloved black kettle is one of smaller size, suitable for insertion into the pot-hole of the kitchen stove, in which any eventually palatable green bean must be cooked, with a slab of meat, long enough to insure the penetration into every pod of a truly ineffable flavor and the extermination of every lurking vitamin. The very thought of it makes us as nostalgic in our way as those naturewriters who went to Times Square and made good are in theirs. . . .

December 8, 1944

The 1938 Hurricane

A tropical hurricane roared across New England on the night of September 21, 1938, following three days of heavy rain. Convocation, scheduled for the next morning, was canceled. Although no college buildings were damaged, the loss of giant elm and pine trees all over town was calamitous.

The 170th year of Dartmouth College did not come in like a lamb. It came in with a combination of flood and hurricane and it was, all in all, rather terrifying.

On Wednesday afternoon there was nothing more noteworthy about the new college year than that it was receiving a rather damp birth. Good old Hanover Plain was pretty well soaked through by two weeks of intermittent downpour. Mink Brook was tearing noisily down to the Connecticut like an overgrown youth who doesn't know his own strength, and hundreds of rivulets were pouring down the slopes from the College Plain to the river, which was growing ominously large. The freshmen, except for a half dozen who were delayed for various reasons, were all safely registered and matriculated and were busily engaged, in between thunder showers, in efforts to dash desks, chairs, and mattresses to their rooms without getting completely soaked in the process. The vanguard of the upperclassmen had already arrived and begun to register on Wednesday. For two weeks the Big Green had been going through its paces on turf that became soggier and soggier as the days passed and had begun to take on a distinctly over-ripe odor, to the extent that Harry Ellinger, while declaring that he had never been over-hesitant about rubbing his own face in gridiron mud or asking his charges to do this, began to grant a justifiable reluctance in this regard.

Webster Hall on Wednesday afternoon was ready for the opening exercises scheduled for nine o'clock the following morning and President Hopkins had prepared the material for another informal opening address, following the experiment of last years' informal opening which was so popular with the undergraduates. As the dinner hour approached, the white tower of Baker stood out against a grey and lowering sky and a gusty, petulant wind blew rain in the faces of the freshmen on their way to the Commons. The noon radio reports had indicated that the tropical hurricane which wandered out to sea from its usual path across Florida would probably strike along the New England Coast, and a few weather-wise housewives brought in the Monday wash which had been getting wetter daily. People were preparing for a bit of a blow.

But no one was prepared for the hell that broke loose a few minutes before six o'clock. One was surprised suddenly to observe a towering elm stretched across the road with its torn roots reaching six or eight feet into the air. Incredulity mounted as with a strange silentness, because nothing could be heard through the deep roar of the growing wind, other trees dropped here, there, and in all directions. Soon town lights were out and all but College buildings, getting their electricity underground from the college plant, were plunged into darkness. Telephones were dead. As the darkness grew the wind intensified and by eight o'clock a hurricane was roaring such as none who had never lived in or near the tropics had ever seen or dreamed of. Gradually the current was cut off from the live wires which had danced wildly about streets sending off showers of fireworks from automobiles and other objects. Onlookers in their respective shelters were completely cut off from all sensations except the roar of the wind and the tremble of buildings as nearby trees fell. The large smokestack at the heating plant swayed dangerously in the wind. Only the illuminated tower of the Library shed light on Hanover as venturesome students gathered in the center of the campus to watch the elms fall around them.

By nine o'clock the wind slackened. There came a lull of fifteen

4. Two scenes of 1938 hurricane damage in the Bema and (below) near Dartmouth Row.

to twenty minutes and then a less severe blow from a different quarter for another hour. Then in the hours before midnight the population of the town ventured forth with flashlights to see the unbelievable things about them. Students with never-failing energy came forth, under the direction of Palaeopitus and the Outing Club, to begin the work of clearing roads. There were probably few, if any, blocks of streets around Hanover and other towns in this area which did not have at least one tree across them.

When the serene sunny day dawned on Thursday it was amazing that traffic could circulate with an occasional detour here and there, thanks to the efforts through the night of workers in clearing pathways through the tangled streets.

It was also amazing how little property was damaged and how giant trees, which would have demolished roofs or done more serious damage if they had fallen a foot or two to the north or south, fell miraculously in such a way as to do no damage to buildings. The only really serious residential damage in Hanover was done to the home of Professor Jones on the Lyme Road, where a falling tree demolished the ell of the house. One of the sights which attracted most visitors on this Thursday morning which was to have seen the opening of the college was the garage of Professor Burton on Occom Ridge which was smashed to splinters and the automobile within it flattened like a pancake. Probably the two most pathetic sights were the College Park and the Cathedral Pines, the latter so carefully preserved for many years by the Pine Park Association on the slopes of the Connecticut. War veterans remarked that many weeks of intense bombardment could not have created such utter chaos as the mellow September sun uncovered on Thursday. Where the generous arching trees of the College Park formerly made a pleasant pattern of sunlight and shade on the Commencement crowds gathered on sparkling June mornings, the Bema's skyline on Thursday morning was only the rugged rocks of hilltop cluttered by fallen tree trunks and huge upturned clumps of roots and earth, accentuated by the sharp stone spear of Bartlett Tower. And on the golf course, where one was accustomed to see the tall crest of pines on the ridge towering against the distant hills of

Norwich, only a half dozen stripped and splintered trunks remained, rising gaunt against the sky and the now desolate hills of Vermont. Those who have known these sights for many years dropped unashamed tears with the realization that Hanover, as they had previously known it, would never look the same again in their lifetime or probably in the lifetimes of their sons.

Perhaps all this sounds rather dramatic, and it was dramatic. However, one should not visualize an unrecognizable Hanover. The percentage of trees which fell around the campus and the town, apart from concentrated havoc in the College Park and in the Pine Park, was not very great and while there will be discernible gaps—as for instance where the enormous elm fell across Main Street onto the portico of College Hall, and other big elms fell here and there around the green—the town is by no means bereft of trees and one quickly becomes accustomed to the changes that have been wrought. . . .

It was only those farther south who suffered from the swollen rivers, except for the interruption of railroad schedules. For two days Hanover was almost completely cut off from the outside world, with all railroad operations completely discontinued and automobile traffic difficult and uncertain, where possible at all. The long distance telephone service was entirely cut off; Western Union was neither sending nor receiving messages, and there was none except local mail service. It was all, however, more a matter of inconvenience than of actual distress. There were no real shortages in supplies and after the excitement of the first day, with the surprising resiliency of which people seem to be capable in time of emergency, life went on much as before.

October 1, 1938

The Fifth-Down Game

The famous Dartmouth-Cornell "fifth-down game" was played in Hanover on November 16, 1940. Cornell's winning touchdown was scored in the closing seconds, but upon postgame disclosure that the Ithacans had been given an extra fifth down in their scoring series, Cornell declined the victory and conceded that Dartmouth had won, 3–0.

"SOME DAY the fires will doubtless burn far into the night—at Syracuse, Columbus, Morningside, New Haven, Hanover, or Philadelphia—in honor of the excellent and inspired eleven which smote the Cornell football team of 1940 on all its tenderest and most exposed portions with everything it could lay its hands on, from the water-bucket to pieces of the south goalposts."—Romeyn Berry in the CORNELL ALUMNI NEWS, quoted in Bulletin No. 7.

That day was yesterday and the place was Hanover. Even the prophetic Mr. Berry did not foresee that the day would be a Monday and not a Saturday. Not a "blue Monday," but a Red Monday, a Green Monday, a Green-and-Red Monday like Christmas and all other festivals rolled into one. And even though the excitement found expression in three celebrations in one evening—Captain Lou Young borne down Main Street on the shoulders of students for once unashamed of enthusiasm, throngs explosive with joyous excitement calling the Big Green, man by man from training table in the Inn; a descent upon the President's house, demanding that he be summoned home from a dinner party (with the Dartmouth Defense Group and Palaeopitus, at the Outing Club House), demanding "The balcony! the balcony!" when he undertook to speak from the front steps (necessitating the prying open of a window never opened before), heckling happily and cheering at every fourth word, crying, "Holiday! Holiday!" (to no avail); moving on to Dean Neidlinger's crying "Holiday! Holiday!" (to no avail); forcing a padlock protecting the Rollins chimes, and enlivening the third celebration, at midnight, with two fire alarms—even though the general delight and merriment found its expression in the foregoing, and other, phenomena, the one thing almost forgotten were the bonfires prophesied by Mr. Berry. But they were remembered finally, at divers times and in divers places. It was, all in all, the biggest celebration ever held in Hanover. It dwarfed the celebration of the first victory over Yale. It was something enormous.

There are two things to be remembered before going into detail about the magnificent Dartmouth team which rose up and smote the great and invincible Cornellians, shackled their vaunted attack, pushed their All-Americans around Memorial Field; about the 3–0 victory won on Krieger's field goal, about the touchdown won by a Cornell team also suddenly magnificent on what proved to be a fifth down, as the big clock showed 0 seconds to play; about the referee's subsequent acknowledgement of error and apology; about Cornell's handsome generosity and sportsmanship in giving Dartmouth an official victory which Dartmouth had handsomely won but which only Cornell could give; and about the Hanover celebrations.

The first thing to be remembered is that this Dartmouth team *was* magnificent. In all the excitement about fifth downs, an historic referee's recantation, a precedent-shattering opponent's concession of victory, people have forgotten that the really historic thing in this picture was the play of the Big Green on Saturday. People have forgotten the feats of this team of iron men (six played the entire sixty minutes, three played fifty or more, only the ends got real reliefs from the grueling play). People have forgotten the ferocious tackles, the indomitable spirit of men taken out by one block, taken out by a second block, and coming up again to stretch out an arm and

5. Coach Earl Blaik, John Koslowski (33), and Harry Gerber (74) watch from the sidelines as Cornell makes its final drive in the famous fifth-down game of November 16, 1940. Below: Headlines the following Tuesday proclaim a reversal of the victory, with Dartmouth the winner, 3–0.

grab the runner's shoes; the ends who spilled two interferers at once, dammed a third behind this log jam, and slowed the runner for a tackle from behind; the flank defenders who miraculously knifed through a swarm of interferers to snag the runner on the vaunted Big Red end sweeps. They forget the surge of the Green line, irresistible and tireless; Drahos being pushed aside to make holes for Wolfe and Hall; the infinitesimal Arico, looking barely twice as high as the numerals 62 on his back, bowling over Cornellians like tenpins, fighting for the extra half-yard. People forget these things, and they oughtn't to.

The other thing to be remembered is the sportsmanship of Cornell. The *Bulletin* is pleased to have inserted last week's paragraph pointing to the length and the pleasantness of the relationship with Cornell, soliciting sportsmanship and generosity among the Dartmouths in contemplation of Cornell's gridiron prowess. Because the Cornells have indeed been sporting and generous and above reproach on their end. Coach Snavely's telegram to Coach Blaik is as true a keynote as any: "I accept the final conclusions of the officials and without reservation concede the victory to Dartmouth with hearty congratulations to you and the gallant Dartmouth team." After the last whistle blows the game and the score are beyond the control of the officials, and there is nothing in the code to permit the reversal of an official's ruling having any effect on the score after the game's end. Only Cornell could take the token of official victory from herself and give it to Dartmouth. Cornell has done a great deal for amateur sport, for football, for the Ivy League, and for the praise of her own fair name in making this gesture in this generous spirit. The editorial pages of both the NEW YORK TIMES and the NEW YORK HERALD TRIBUNE commented on this subject this morning; doubtless reams will be written on it before time finally dims this unique event in football history, and we of Dartmouth shouldn't forget it in the excitement of the moment.

As for the game itself, keynotes galore can be found. Arico, who was in briefly but explosively, could provide one. On one occasion this midget, with two tacklers already engaged in the time-consuming task of persuading him that he couldn't go any farther, found Finneran, towering Cornell center, in his path and just bowled him over backwards, as simple as that. . . . It was hard for the Cornells to persuade Wolfe not to run any farther, too. This durable, indefatigable back also had a big day. . . . Sometimes Ray Hall looked like Colby Howe, shooting through the off-tackle holes that opened in the line. And for sixty minutes he was in the fray, punting beautifully almost always under fourth-down pressure, aiming true for the corner, away from the eager arms of Landsberg. . . . Norton spent an unsung sixty minutes, calling signals, throwing blocks, pounding in with scrimmage-line tackles as backer-up. . . . A similar role for Kast, whose running plays didn't get away for much yardage. His was the indispensable pass interception of the six-yard line that thwarted one threatening thrust. . . . And what a honey was that interception of Wolfe's in the end zone, a high, one-handed basketball catch on the dead run. The movies of that moment are already worn out, in an effort to analyze the miracle. . . . The ends were alert and insatiable for tackles—Krieger, Crowley, Kelley and Gerber—especially Krieger, who also kicked those three points, after all. . . . The line was just superb. . . . Hickey went in briefly for Crego: otherwise it was an iron-man line for sixty bruising minutes, Pearson, Dacey, Winship and Young. . . . The rangy Pearson, in the process of being taken out of one play by a charging Cornellian, stretched out a large but alert paw that deflected and ruined one of Cornell's dangerous short passes. . . . Young is, by all accounts, a peerless captain. He looks like one, and those who ought to know say he is one. When his team lined up on the defense, he didn't waste any much-needed energy pounding the pants of his teammates. While Cornell huddled, he sauntered out in front of the team, faced them and just talked to them. . . . They say that some of the defensive signals Young called didn't mean anything, but were just meant to baffle and annoy the Cornellians. . . . It seems also that this iron Green team didn't take the contest with any gloomy seriousness, but found occasion for raillery with the Cornells, who were taken a bit by surprise.

Though Dartmouth substantially outmarched Cornell on the ground and showed offensive strength, the great Green accomplishment was stopping the famed Ithacan attack cold, keeping the Big Red inside its own forty-yard line for a whole half, shackling the running game tight and, except for the end of game flurry, keeping the passes well in check. The football savants are calling Dartmouth's defense, which we are too innocent of football science to discuss, a triumph of coaching strategy. Devised by Earl Blaik and colleagues, practiced for ten days, it worked. How it worked! It stopped cold a football machine which had been rolling for the greater part of three seasons, grinding many a formidable opponent under on the way. Defensive play seldom has any color, but this defense was spectacularly colorful.

This game will be talked about for years, so this ought to be enough for this time.

MORE ABOUT THE CELEBRATION

The first celebration took place Saturday at dinner time. The official score was still Cornell 7 – Dartmouth 3; many of the players were borne down by disappointment and the incredible frustration of those last three seconds, but their admiring supporters felt they had something to celebrate, gathered at the Inn corner in unappeasable numbers and demanded the members of the team. They came out.

Yesterday things started brewing as the news began to percolate about that Lynah and Snavely had gracefully thrown the victory pass back to McCarter and Blaik. There was horseplay in the light practice on Memorial Field, but the varsity who looked like Titans on the field on Saturday looked like very young, very light-spirited, very un-brawny kids as they gathered with soap-shiny faces and slick wet hair to look at the movies. The coaches ran the high spots backwards and forwards, found little to criticize!

First celebration boiled up at the Inn corner at the dinner hour. "The full, roaring shout of Dartmouth victory—pent up for two days—thundered across the Hanover plain last night," writes THE DARTMOUTH. The Daily got out an *Extra* which is a saga in itself. By a generous deal, consummated while excitement was at its height, when over 3,000 copies had been printed and still customers crowded the shop, we ordered copies for the *Bulletin*, enclosed herewith. . . . The *Bulletin* ought to be back to normal next week.

November 19, 1940

Pearl Harbor

Little brown men in big planes stinging the big gray battlewagons at dawn in the quiet harbor . . . The sharp electric reflex in a billion billion waves, burning through the Sabbath atmosphere of a spacious continent, bringing a welter of angry feelings somberly touched with apprehension to Californians going to church . . . bringing the embattled world suddenly to the Sunday dinner tables of Middle Westerners, evaporating the mirage of security which an instant earlier lulled the central plains . . . bringing a confusion of emotions to the pits of the stomachs of two-and-a-half thousand college boys in a serene New England village. Undergraduate journalists dash from their radios through the brisk December afternoon to the loose-jointed typewriters in their disordered offices, and thence to the clutter and clatter of the composing room, submerging speculation on the clamoring immediacy of the future in the excitement of getting out an extra . . .

Little brown men in big planes, stinging America. Bright, tough, ingratiating, ridiculous, incredible little begoggled brown men, burning with zeal in their big planes to die gloriously for the Son of Heaven, pouring death out of the skies on sturdy youths in whom burns only the hope of a world where white men, and black men, and little brown men in their rice fields and factories may live in peace and justice. Where hope burns, now also burns anger. Later will come hate, must come hate, at the burn of bullet in flesh, at the fresh earth on a comrade's grave . . .

At the vesper hour on this fateful Sabbath in a hushed goat room, brothers and initiates take reciprocal vows of enduring friendship. One remembers the time when one of the kneeling initiates bore the proud name of the soaring snowy mountain which graces a thousand Japanese prints, a gay and charming companion who fought with courage and skill in the prize ring, played with devastating finesse at the card table, drank with wit and merriment in the tap room, showered gifts upon his hosts, and left a record of brilliant scholarship in the class room . . . our Little Brown Brother whom we vowed to honor and defend, and he us, whatever might betide . . .

As the second day dawned on smoking barracks and burning oil stores in the broad Pacific, the stars of the same tense Sunday shine on a noble New Hampshire hilltop. Carsful of students climb the forbidding grades to the hilltop lodge for the initiation banquet. It is cold . . . Gaiety is overloud at cocktails. In a quiet corner the senior from Chicago is saying that he thinks he will join the air force in February. He says it as if he were saying that he thought he would take Classical Civilization next semester. The junior from Chicago says he thinks he will too. The sophomore from Honolulu doesn't say anything . . . After salad, one slips from the table, then another, then another and another. They are all around the radio in the next room. First Elmer Davis, then Walter Winchell, then more news flashes . . . The rangy senior whose draft deferments have been uncertain all fall—his third season as varsity end—sits with poker face. Nobody says anything. The air is thick with wood smoke, cigarette smoke, and a sense of history. Each reads his future in the crackling flames of the broad fireplace . . . After coffee the chapter president greets the new delegation, the tall blond from Buffalo speaks for the new brothers in 100 seconds, the chapter adviser speaks for two minutes, the brother from Williams for one. The toast is drunk, and that is all . . . Out with frosty breath under the cold bright stars, and back home to the radio and the bull sessions and the wonderings where they will be six months from now . . .

Little brown men in big planes . . .

On Monday, at 12:30 the restaurants, usually thronged at this hour, are all but empty as the President addresses Congress. After lunch, an effigy of Hirohito blossoms out of a second-story window in South Mass., complete with horn-rimmed glasses and a splotch of red on his chest. Next door, in Middle Mass., tiny Takanobu

Mitsui '43, the College's only Japanese citizen, quietly goes about his business, suffering no scarcity of friendship—son of Takanaga Mitsui '15, of one of Japan's great families, tracing back to the 13th century and thence, through the mists of legend, to the gods of the Rising Sun . . . Everyone has his latest news flash, whether fresh from the radio or at garbled fourth hand from the street corner. But there is no news.

Little brown men in big planes, busy about the broad Pacific . . . "ENEMY PLANES OFF SAN FRANCISCO" is the streamer on Tuesday morning's *Dartmouth* . . . "CAPITOL CALM AS PRESIDENT ASKS FOR WAR" . . . " 'WITHOUT QUESTION' JAPANESE WILL LOSE—PROFESSOR LATTIMORE" . . . "COLLEGE CHEST COLLECTS $523 ON FIRST DAY" . . . "UPPER GILE DOWNS WHEEELER 29-0 TO BECOME DORM 'B' FOOTBALL CHAMPIONS" . . . President Hopkins, acting for the Board of Trustees, announces acceptance of recommendations of the Committee on Educational Policy, providing means by which students called before the end of this semester can obtain credits for their courses, and by which seniors, called before the end of the year, may qualify for their degrees. For this semester, it means, through prompt notification of the Dean, arrangement of special written or oral examinations. For seniors, it means the arrangement of special comprehensive examinations, and if possible a month's devotion to preparation for them "to the exclusion of class attendance and extra-curriculum activities." "A senior anticipating induction at the end of the first semester shall complete his regular courses before entering upon the intensive period of preparation for the comprehensive examinations. He may do so as provided . . . above by special course examinations." . . . "A student who completes the courses of the first semester and passes a special examination as described above will be recommended for the Bachelor of Arts degree without being required to complete the normal course requirements of the second semester." The latter means that a senior in these circumstances would be excused from the normal two second-semester courses outside of his major subject . . . At the concert, Conductor Iturbi raises his baton and says: "Will you join us in *The Star-Spangled Banner*." There is a special tingle to singing it, with a symphony orchestra, at this hour . . . As the last note of the second encore dies away, a loudspeaker is brought on the stage and the President's fireside chat begins. When it is over, there is clapping, and people leave, saying it was a good speech, and feeling just a little let down, that there was no news of the events at Pearl Harbor, that it didn't quite ring the bell.

But the bell had already been rung, by little brown men in big planes, fifty hours before . . .

Wednesday, Thursday, and Friday pass. Germany and Italy and a degraded herd of stooge governments declare war on the United States, and it all seems as stale as last Thursday's *Boston Herald*. The basketball team wins its opening game from the University of Vermont, and the fact is lost in the streaming headlines. The flag in front of Dartmouth Hall is half-masted for three days, signifying the end of life for Sidney Lane Smith '43, who died where he wanted to be, where doctors told him he should not be, in his dormitory room at Dartmouth College—incurably and hopelessly ill with nephritis, painfully crippled, but endowed with a burning intelligence and a flaming courage, he entered college against medical advice, was forced out by serious aggravation of his illness, returned on the strength of his will and his courage, and died no doubt as he wished and perhaps as he expected to die, in his dormitory bed . . .

Wednesday's issue of *The Dartmouth* reports that William F. Abrams '44 has left to join the Marines—the first to go since the declaration of war. The students are talking, talking, wondering, feeling a latent need for action, hoping for guidance and leadership out of their confusion. The lines are long outside the Dean's office, including many who are expecting early induction, or think they ought to expect it, and are trying to prepare for early completion of their course requirements according to the new provisions described above. But there is yet no sign that the draft boards will emerge soon from their own confusion and lack of knowledge concerning what they must expect, sufficiently to guide students who are subject to call . . . Dartmouth Broadcasting System announces it is taking its newcasts off the air, in compliance with President Roosevelt's request for an end to rumor-mongering . . . President

Hopkins joins Professors Wilson, Sikes, McDaniel, and Bannerman in a panel discussion in the course on Democratic Thought, answering student questions largely in the field of economic democracy. The students are worried that democracy is always put to initial disadvantage by the authoritarian power to take the initiative, wonder if democracy must always submit to the staggering first blow. The panel leaders sharply bring into focus the fact that democracy can live only by adherence to its principles—but that the strength of democracy, while slow in rising, is sure and overpowering when aroused . . . The student next to us heads his notebook page simply: "December 12——Hoppy" . . . Again we think, in contemplating the probable rise of excess nationalism and even jingoism under war psychology, how much more valid is the solid grounding provided by a course like this in what democracy fundamentally is, where it came from, where with wisdom it may go, inside and beyond the horizons of America . . . and how essential is such knowledge if we are to win the peace after we win the war . . .

On Friday word came that the men who jointly wrote Monday's editorial, the editor-in-chief and the editorial chairman,* left College on Tuesday, made the rounds of the recruiting offices of the Navy, the Coast Guard, the Marines, and the Air Corps, and at length managed to pass the visual requirements of the Army and there enlisted. Most of their friends thought this not as wise as finishing their semester, or even the year, but respected the strength of their convictions . . . *The Importance of Being Earnest*, in the Little Theatre Friday evening, is deft and amusing, in pointed contrast, in its decadence and wit, to the times . . . Unconfirmed reports place Lieutenant Don Otis '37 in charge of a detachment of Marines on the heroic acres of Wake Island . . .

On Saturday evening a special faculty meeting. Extra chairs—the largest attendance in years. President Hopkins explains the purpose of the meeting and calls on Professor Scarlett, chairman of the Com-

---

*The editor-in-chief was Jerry Tallmer '42, who writes for the *New York Post*, and the editorial chairman was Alex Fanelli '42, who is executive assistant to President Kemeny.

mittee on Educational Policy, for the recommendations from the committee, arrived at the day previously after a joint session with the Committee on Defense Instruction, the President and the Deans: compression of the second semester, closing with Commencement on May 10, five weeks ahead of schedule. The same amount of work to be done: 41 class exercises instead of 42. First and second semester examination schedules are compressed (using evenings and Sundays), February and Easter recesses eliminated, the social functions of Carnival cancelled, the slack tightened all along the line. The purpose: To accelerate the completion of educational units while maintaining the validity of the work done, preparing men earlier for military induction without loss of academic credit, for summer work in industry and education, or for summer schools toward earlier degrees. It recognizes the importance attached by most of the military services to the completion of educational units, particularly in candidates for commissions. There is also an anticipated psychological advantage in this intensification of work, toward decreased restlessness . . . An amendment is proposed doing away with comprehensive examinations, which is briefly discussed and voted down . . . Then the Committee's recommendations are voted, unanimously . . . The meeting is closed, and the persisting sense of history is strong . . . The action leaves a wake of problems: for the D.O.C. (loss of Carnival income, etc., etc.), for the Commencement Committee (what *will* a May 10 Commencement be like, anyway), for the Alumni Council (what will happen to class reunions?), and a host of others . . . Also it raises anew, in a fresh light of importance, the question of a summer semester . . .

So a historic week draws to its close, and snow falls . . . Snow falls abundantly, inexorably, continuingly, blanketing the Hanover earth as hundreds of millions of free men and more who hope to be free will blanket the yellow shadow cast by little brown men in big planes, the retching saffron shadow thrown in hate across the globe by the little brown-shirted psychopath with the silly mustache . . . Through the deep Hanover snow, into the hushed candlelight of garlanded Rollins Chapel, troop the community, bringing a multitude of little ones, for the Christmas Carol service

6. The special Convocation of January 1942 at which President Hopkins announced war plans to accelerate the college year and hold Commencement in May.

on Sunday afternoon . . . In the evening, a multitude of students troop over the same paths, now well worn, for their special carol service. President Hopkins in the pulpit. In misty candlelight in the back of the chapel is the Prokofieff Orchestra and the Handel Singers. In the choir box, framed by boughs and candelabra, is the glee club against a deep red backdrop. "When a thousand voices sang," a student writes, "the uneasiness of a College at war faded . . . The most important thing . . . was the pause from restlessness, a unity, and a momentary enlargement of the present—the calm of Christmas." . . . The carol service is a thing of loveliness, of the quiet hope and faith which is the happiness of troubled times.

In mid-morning Monday the President calls the College into a special convocation. Faculty and an overflow of students fill Webster's stage, the students fill every crevice of the hall, and overflow with faculty wives into the chapel to listen to an amplifying extension. The President describes the calendar revision, and its purposes . . . "Work will be intensive and continuous for the students, and those who teach them" . . . "The C man should remember that the College record is first criterion examined for military and naval commissions and officers' training courses" . . . "Carnival is out" . . . "Easter vacation is out" . . . "Premature enlistments already resulting in advancements denied" . . . "Deep importance of a liberal education in a postwar world" . . . "This is not the least fortunate of generations" . . . "'Don't be tragic" . . . "Don't sap vitality with melancholy" . . . "It is not necessary to throw away all the keys of happiness to wage war successfully." . . . As the undergraduates file out, the seed of hysteria is dead, feet are again on the ground, they are their jest-loving selves again. "Happy Easter!" they call to each other on the way to class.

December 15, 1951

Our Hopes for 1943 for You, for Dartmouth, and for V

We greet the New Year full of hope
For freedom's gain, and enough rope
To those who seared the world in hate
And in its rage now read their fate.
And, never loath to imitate
Sullivan, Joyce Kilmer, or the Pope
We loosely rhyme, with goodwill great,
In lines that, may they limp or lope
In verse form well beyond our scope
Yet bear, to thee, and thee, and thee,
Best hopes for 1943
From us (The Bull. and A.I.D.)
For you, for Dartmouth and for V!

(For anti-climax prize, we hail:
"For God, for Country, and for Yale")

The choicest garlands from the Elm
Endow the brow at Dartmouth's helm:
Loud may the Big Green praises pop
For him we know and love as Hop.
Cheers too—the fustest and the mostest—
For Prexy's helpmate, Dartmouth's hostess.
For Ann, and Ensign John Rust Potter
We bless the hearth of Hoppy's daughter:
A wah-hoo-wah for grandsons lusty
For Martin Hopkins and for Rusty.

Hail, all who wear the Green or khaki
In Africa, and on Tulagi.
With pride we chant our greetings loud
To Colby Howe and Bob MacLeod,
To Connor, Inglehart and Blethen,
All leathernecks who scorch the heathen.
To Chippy Semmes and armored son
A Nazi goose, not too well done.
To Riflemen Bolte and Durkee
A cheer for basting Rommel's turkey.
All Dartmouth men in Franklin's fleet
From gob to captain, praises greet.
A flame in Dartmouth hearts will burn
In memory of Charlie Stern.
To Airmen Eaton and Carruthers
Greetings—and four thousand others.

A cheer, impertinent and fearless
To Richardsons, Big Jim and Cheerless.
May measured coolth and rationed hunger
Avoid Al Foley, Dow and Unger.
We, unrepentant, greet the wayward
Secretary-General Hayward,
And roguishly embrace the wrong
Exampled in Dean Robert Strong.
May candid phrase and contract skill
Still fill the days of Gordon Bill.

For Neidlingers—gals, Pudge and Trot
Be New Year's fortune not forgot.
To Neef, Armbruster Francis Joe
A lot of joy, a lack of woe.
McCallum lank and Schlossie spherical;
A New Year gay if not hysterical.
For Stearns and Messer only seek
Such blessings as were named by Greek.

To Edgerton, Don Barr, and Norton
To Conant, R., and Dr. Horton,
To Gooding, Porter, Olmsted, West,
Widmayer, C.,—we wish the best.
To Proctor, Hull, Frey, Murch and Keir
To Scarlett, Skinner—all good cheer.

To Coburn (Miss) and Hancock, too,
The thanks of him whose work they do.
Commander Coyle and Captain Tanzer:
Anesthetize the Nip and Panzer!
For neuro-surgeon Captain Heyl
"Sieg Heil"—were puns and heils in style.
Intelligencers Hurd and Diller:
Out-cerebrate the Axis killer!
For Private Cobleigh on this day
The *Halls of Montezuma* play.
Let not with undue thorns the path
Be strewn for French profs boning math.
In physics labs, ungird the heart
For harassed profs of Greek and Art;
But this is war, Professor Murch—
So praise the Lord—and pass the birch!

We welcome, on our sea of snow
The Navy—Lads! Look out below!
Let's pipe aboard the College Hall
The Skipper, students, gobs and all;
A campus hornpipe, if you please,
For Captain Briggs' indoctrinees.

Milk and honey, all that's good
To Barbara and Harvey Hood.
All that's good and scads of money
To Chairman Atwood—skip the honey.
Out loudest greetings, meek yet lusty

To every gent entitled Trustee.
Our warmest wishes loudest chant
To Rockefeller, Gile and Grant.
To Cutters and aforesaid Hoodsies
All the best in worldly goodsies.
May tax and ration fail to pinsch
Orr and Ruggles, French and Minsch.
(To Sullivan, we add a dash
Of daffy versifier Nash)
Blast misfortune, banish bane,
From all the clan that's high McLane.

To Carl F. Woods, to Tuss McLaughry
The novum annum's richest dowry.
To Dartmouth's foundling, Corey Ford,
The boon of classmates' high regard.
To all the Larmons—Sig and Russell,
Kath and Kitty—tidings hustle.
To Hubbells—offspring, Jack and Ruth—
A nifty '43, forsooth.
To Frank Drake and to Gulf garages
A wistful glance—they're just mirages.
To Sterlings, "hats all in the ring,"
The best that '43 can bring.
To C.H.S. of '79
We only wish the superfine.
To Harry Gilmore, C. McDavitt
Our praise—well may they have it.
To Abel, Castle, Brown and Oakes
To all the other Dartmouth folks;
To Mackey, Huck, Rourke, Knibbs, all Perry's
To Geller, Holton and Bud Walls
A '43 that's just the berries
A '43 that never palls.
With Reynolds, Frank, of '89
We mull a mug of warming wine.

Greet Reynolds, James, of '90's corps:
No man has youth or humor more.
To Orsi, Lanes and Timbers three
The maximum of jollity.
For Sheldon, Seney, Frederick, Tindle
Some extra thermal units kindle.
To Montross, F. and Hotchkiss, Gene
An extra gill of gasoline.
From brimming cup, we down a snootful
In tribute to the Horans fruitful.
Greet Philip Sanford Marden who's
Majestic in both mien and prose.
To Parker Hayden, Spider Martin
All blessings that are good and sartin.
To Cunninghams, both Bill and Don,
Fitzgerald, H. and Remsen, John,
MacMannis, Bert and Thurber, G.
The utmost health and wealth and glee.
To Pritchard, R. and Loudon, pink,
The utmost good that we can think.
For Baldwin, Moore and Flanigan
We hope God does the best He can.
For Louer, Weymouth and McFarland
We lovingly entwine a garland.
For Pleasants and George Maurice Morris
We gaily lift a doch-an-dorris.
For host at Hotel View-of-Mountain
One empty room to Dodge around in.
For Soldier Ford and Peggy Sayre
Proximity to make life gayre.
Endow with goods surpassing need
All Emersons of Dartmouth breed.
To Mathes, Inc. and each relation
The joys of pin-point carbonation.

To Ensigns Foley, Cohen, King
To Palamountain, too, we sing,
To Zimmerman, the Loot. Commander
Lieutenant Osgood, Ensign Chandler
Lieutenant Smith, all boys in blue
And to the lads in khaki, too.
To Wainwright, French, and Rauch, Lieutenants
And Horn and Denny, wave the pennants.
Hail, mighty midget, Major South
Who lays the eggs on pigboats' snouts.
Ex-roommates Low, McClellan, Troy
We wish an increment of joy.

For Woosters, let's remove the cork
And toast their double-barrelled stork.
To Lizzy, Phil, and Johnny Peck
We pledge in bubble-water, sec.
To Chilcote, Shultz, Borella, Cole
Let's elevate the flowing bowl.
For Haffenreffers, Carl and Carol,
Pete and Ginny, roll the barrel!
To Bowes, to Burns, to Meyers (Pooch)
We pledge a toast in festive hooch.
McDonough, Jeremiah, Faust
The Tangemen, Elas—give a roust!
To Celie and the guy named Warren
A mausoleum to stow their car in.
To Bassett, Richards, Scribner, Bowlen,
Four beds of roses just to roll in.
To all the brood, both clean and dirty,
Our love to *all* the class of '30.

May Doc O'Connor through many a day
Eschew those rooms where doctors play.
To Warren Kendall, Arthur Cohen,
Ben Ames Williams, Carl M. Owen,
Thurlow Gordon, Leslie Snow,
Coulson, Mason, Johnson, Low,
To Abbott, Embree (nicknames: Bill);
All Wheelockmen, our beakers fill!

Now friends, if we have missed a man
It is because his name won't scan.
Each auld acquaintance we'd fain include
(More friends to say our verse is good)
But, be your view we shine or smell,
We everlasting wish you well;
And if you blindly think we stink,
Your just reward the New Year brink.

December, 1942

4. Admissions

Mr. Dickerson served as Director of Admissions from 1946 to 1956. For the latter half of that period he also served as Chairman of the Committee on Scholarships and Loans and Chairman of the Committee on Admission and the Freshman Year. For the final two years, 1954–56, he was on leave from his admissions post in order to serve as Executive Director of the Trustees Planning Committee, appointed by the Trustees to make plans for the decade leading up to Dartmouth's bicentennial in 1969.

"Enter Ye in by the Narrow Gate..."

An article explaining Dartmouth admissions policies and problems, written by Mr. Dickerson, then director of admissions, for the October 1947 issue of the Dartmouth Alumni Magazine.

"You and your boy should understand," the admissions officer was saying, "the competitive situation which a boy faces for college admission today. Take, for example, our 6000 applicants for 650 places this year. The competition is pretty keen. On the other hand, we must not let it appear so fantastically difficult to get into college that even good men will not try. I know of no college which is in imminent danger of enrolling a freshman class composed exclusively of supermen."

"Well," said the father, taking a long look into the eyes of his son, "seventeen is no age at which to start running away from competition."

The boy nodded, a little shyly, more than a little eagerly.

This is not a parable. It is a fragment of conversation which actually took place day before yesterday, which has had hundreds and hundreds of counterparts in recent months.

Fact or parable, it could serve in itself as a fair summary of the problem of college admission today, or it could serve as the text of a really exhaustive, definitive exposition of the numerous facets of college admission problems.

This present piece will not stop with the text. Neither can it, within the space which the editor can devote to it and within the fifteen or twenty minutes which readers might be willing to spend on it, undertake the definitive treatment.

Consider even a fragmentary listing of the facets which an exhaustive exposition of admission might include.

It might include consideration of Dartmouth's relationships with the College Entrance Examination Board system, past and potential. This would be a major treatise in itself. It might include a diatribe on the "first choice" shibboleth which some colleges in our group apply, and which the College Entrance Examination Board aids and abets in the face of a rising resentment among the schools and their students—a resentment against its unfairness in these times when a boy just can't "choose" his college. A definitive document might include treatment of the unparalleled participation of Dartmouth alumni in recruiting and evaluating candidates for admission, but that also would require a long, long chapter. There might be consideration of preparation for Dartmouth, with some discussion of public versus private schools; and as the converse of the competition for admission, there might be examination of the competition among the colleges for the best men in the schools, which would get us into the whole realm of college public relations.

And so on. But before I become like the anesthetic orator who exhausts his hearers with a forty-minute summary of things he is not going to talk about, I proceed with the immediate subject of this piece, which is: (1) the setting of college admissions today; (2) the principles of Dartmouth's Selective Process; (3) a sketchy outline of its procedures; and (4) a consideration of the status of sons of Dartmouth men applying for admission.

THE SETTING

"Enter ye in by the narrow gate . . . and few be they that find it," say the Scriptures.

The portals of the colleges and universities today are indeed narrow in proportion to the number seeking entrance. The absolute good required to pass through the straitened way of Matthew's gospel is a little different from the virtue required for those who

7. A photograph of Al Dickerson taken in 1946 when he was named Director of Admissions.

seek to wind over the ever broader and smoother roads provided by the New Hampshire Highway Commission. These latter travellers meet only relative—i.e., *competitive*—standards. But the competition is rugged enough.

We cannot complain, because Dartmouth introduced the now prevalent competitive elements into college admissions. Having made this bed, we must lie in it with all possible grace, however fitfully admissions officers may sleep in it.

An eminent headmaster was reflecting the other day on the competitive nature of college admissions and the difficulty of educating the public to this fact. "Up to 25 years ago," he recalled, "all you had to do was pick your college, 'pass' the College Boards with the equivalent of the grade of C, and you were in. Then you people at Dartmouth introduced your selective process as a more adequate basis for selecting students from the enormously increasing number of applicants. Now all the colleges are doing just about the same thing. But people don't realize what a *competitive* business it is, and it's going to take years to educate them."

Although we may claim, with currently restrained enthusiasm, to have "invented" the competitive system of selection, we can certainly claim no monopoly on it now. Colleges which before the war were paying agents in the field five or ten dollars a head for freshmen are now looking down their lengthening noses with some hauteur at candidates who hesitate to swear on a mountain of Bibles that Blank College has been their dearest aim since birth. Historic liberal arts colleges such as Princeton, Harvard, Amherst, Williams and Yale, are in the same boat with us. Such published statistics on applications in relation to openings as I have seen quote Dartmouth with the highest ratio, but these are necessarily loose statistics, and all these colleges are undoubtedly in very similar positions.

Statements have been pouring from the various college campuses, seeking public understanding of the problem and, more particularly, the understanding of the respective alumni bodies. Alumni can help: by educating other, less well-informed alumni; by reinforcing the college's public relations which are inevitably strained when only one out of eight or ten applicants is destined to be admitted.

The factors contributing to this enormous bulge of applications are under discussion daily in newspapers and popular magazines and do not need to be reviewed here.

How long will these conditions last? Indefinitely, so far as we can see. Some prognostications say that the crisis will not be reached until 1950, but these relate mainly to enrollments rather than admissions. For colleges like Dartmouth which intend to return to their pre-war enrollments, and to do this by admitting only normal-sized freshman classes, it seems unlikely that the pressure of applications in relation to openings will change materially.

Continued national prosperity (whatever that means, if anything, in these inflated days) and students seeking to escape the congestion of the state universities, which have made such heroic efforts to meet the prodigious obligations thrust upon them, would tend to increase the number of applications to the private colleges where, in varying degrees, expansion has been more controlled. On the other hand, the backlog of veterans has been largely liquidated with the '51 applicants. This group (very largely young veterans with no war experience, treated exactly as all other candidates) included many men who prior to eligibility for G.I. educational benefits, had had no hope or intention of entering college, and were hopelessly unprepared. As a result, whereas about 25% of our '51 applicants were veterans, only about half of this proportion were able to qualify. If a dropping off of applications from this hopelessly unprepared group is to be expected, as I rather believe it is with increasing public understanding of the situation, it will come from the bottom of the list, rather than from the top where the competition exists. So it does not seem likely that the competitive situation will change much in the next few years.

A severe depression or the enactment of a universal military service law might alter the situation, but speculating on these subjects is pure crystal-gazing. The depression of the '30's did not materially affect Dartmouth applications.

I find myself referring to the present fierce competition as "bad" or "worse," because this has become conventional and it comes naturally to an admissions officer struggling to stay on top of his job. Obviously, however, those colleges are most fortunate which have the largest number of applicants to choose from. (Or so we keep reminding ourselves.)

Anyway, for better or for worse, the situation seems unlikely to change much.

PRINCIPLES OF THE SELECTIVE PROCESS

"Has the Dartmouth admissions system changed?" we are often asked.

It has not changed. But the conditions under which it operates have changed enormously, as indicated in the paragraphs above.

The system is very simple, and very flexible. As defined in the minutes of the Board of Trustees, it reads: *All candidates who are admitted to Dartmouth College shall have satisfied the requirements of the Selective Process for admission and shall have presented evidence satisfactory to the Committee on Admissions that they are competent to carry on their course of study at Dartmouth College.*

This simplification, enacted in 1933 after due discussion and endorsement by the faculty, abolished the traditional 15-unit requirement. This was not designed to make it "easier" to get into Dartmouth. It was promulgated at a time when the competition for admission, and the resulting standards, were on a consistent upward curve. Indeed, it recognized the fact that under these rising competitive criteria, the old 15-unit minimum requirements were no longer necessary or useful as a "floor." Also, the increased flexibility made it possible to admit an occasional boy of rare promise who might, for one reason or another, be technically deficient according to the 15-unit provisions.

Year by year there has appeared in the official bulletins of the College—without change, so far as I know, during the 25 years in which the Selective Process has been in operation—an interpretation of its principles. As appearing on Page 41 of Dartmouth College Bulletin Number 4, *Regulations and Courses*, November, 1946, it reads:

Dartmouth holds unreservedly that definite evidence of intellectual capacity is indispensable, but it believes that, after such evidence is established, positive qualities of character and personality, range of interests, and capable performance in outside activities should operate as determining factors in selection. All candidates, therefore, are judged on the basis of the following qualifications:

Scholarship. The record of each candidate for his entire secondary school course is carefully studied with particular emphasis given to the work of the last two years. If a candidate is to be admitted, his scholastic record and the recommendation given to him by his school principal must show that he is possessed of an educational background sufficiently rich and broad in range to indicate definite intellectual capacity and ability to do justice to the academic work of the college. A candidate may present for admission any subjects taught in an approved secondary school which represent accepted courses in the following fields of study: English, Foreign Language (ancient or modern or both), Mathematics, Natural Sciences, Social Studies.

Character and Personality. Character is used to denote such qualities as trustworthiness, initiative, dependability and conscientiousness. The characteristics which are included under the term "personality" are those which lead naturally to some breadth of contact and to some variety of interest. It is understood that the term necessarily deals with intangibles rather than with absolutes. In general, however, it may be said that the man whom the college desires to enroll in its undergraduate membership is the man of intellectual competence and stalwartness of character, if, in addition to these attributes, he possesses likewise the qualities which collectively attract rather than repel the friendship and confidence of others, thus enabling him without sacrificing individuality to cultivate respect and to establish influence among other men.

Groups To Which Preference Is Given

Properly qualified sons of alumni and officers of Dartmouth College, residents of New Hampshire, residents of states west of the Mississippi or south of the Potomac and Ohio Rivers, and residents of territories and dependencies of the United States and of foreign countries, are given some preference at the time of selection. These four groups constitute approximately twenty-five per cent of the entering class.

I don't know whether President Hopkins or Dean Bill, the first director of admissions, originally authored this statement or whether they both contributed to it. But I must record, after a year's rather intensive experience working under this interpretation of the principles of the Selective Process, my respect for its aptness and its adequacy.

As I began to operate in the admissions field, questions arose in my mind at various points concerning the possible desirability of reviewing and perhaps revising some of our procedures. Some of these questions are now under study, and will be considered by the Faculty Committee on Admissions, and discussed with the Alumni Council's Committee on Admissions and Schools. But the more I have worked with our Selective Process, the more respect I have developed for its essential soundness, and the more uncertainty I have whether any significant changes are immediately in order.

For my own guidance, I have tried to supplement the primary interpretation of the Selective Process, as quoted above, with an interpretation of the immediate objectives of the process in terms of Dartmouth's aims and purposes as defined by the President. Basing it on the College's "primary obligation to human society"— a statement by President Hopkins echoing Dr. Tucker's emphasis of "public-mindedness" and strongly restated by President Dickey —there appear to be five points at which the Selective Process should seek to operate toward the fulfillment of this obligation.

(1) Since the possession of a mind is what distinguishes human society from the other primates, the possession of a mind becomes

our first criterion, so that Dartmouth may send forth men with good—and well-trained and well-informed—minds, and with high purposes.

(2) President Dickey has emphasized and re-emphasized, the urgency of the time element at the critical point which human society now faces. As he has said: "There is so little time." Thus it is the obligation of those of us working on admissions to seek with more eagerness than ever *to make every man count*: to seek men who will, in addition to having well-developed mental equipment, have also the drive, the determination, the vigor, the qualities of leadership to make their influence effective.

(3) Assuming that Dartmouth's influences are good, it should be our objective to spread them widely. Men tend to return to their original home communities. Thus we find that the emphasis on geographical distribution becomes, if anything, more significant than ever.

(4) Then there is the diversification of the student body, which is vital to that mutual education which goes on in a college like Dartmouth. You will recall that favorite quotation of President Hopkins about the "impact of youthful mind on youthful mind" as one of the most important parts of the educational process. This is where diversification comes in, so that this mutual impact may be most comprehensive, as men of widely differing backgrounds react upon one another. This diversification should include the geographical distribution mentioned above as well as the broadest possible range of economic, social, religious and occupational backgrounds, so that Dartmouth may continuingly and increasingly represent the whole rich diversity of American life.

This is as good a point as any at which to underline one aspect of this diversification—the range in economic backgrounds. It is profoundly important that Dartmouth should continue to attract the boy of limited means. It is perhaps permissible, in a family organ of this sort, to recognize the fact that this aspect of Dartmouth's constituency is much envied by some of our sister institutions which are much concerned by the great and growing degree to which they draw upon the sons of the upper middle class, as represented, for example, by the high proportion of their men entering from the private schools. The strong pull that Dartmouth has on the best men in the public schools is one of our great assets. And it is going to take watchfulness and real effort to maintain this strength. President Dickey had this very much in mind in his exceedingly careful attention to the public relations aspects of the recent increase in our combined fee, and the strong emphasis put upon the fact that it should not and would not become more difficult for the man of limited means to get a Dartmouth education. But this public relations problem is not one that disappeared at the time of the announcement of the change in the fee: it is a continuing job in which all alumni must actively participate. A fee of $550 looks like quite a lot of money, and it is important to Dartmouth that the promising but impecunious high school graduate in South Dakota should realize that men with minimum financial resources have always been able to get a Dartmouth education, and are still able to do so.

And still further underlining may be appropriate for one particular segment in the group of men of limited means—the marginal man. This is the candidate whose parents, with sacrifices, have always been able to pay for the things they have provided for their children and who might consider it compromising to their self-respect to ask for financial aid. This is a group which, because it is hard to identify, is deserving of our particular attention. It is well for these men to realize that even the student who pays the full fees at Dartmouth is paying only half of the cost of his education.

(5) And now, after diversification of the student body, we come to breadth of interest in the individual man.

This is, if I may startle you with an original observation, a complex world. It is not going to be understood, let alone be influenced, by the one-track person. The really brilliant man, ear-marked as a potential intellect of the first rank can be indulged in some one-sidedness—although, it is to be observed, he seldom is one-sided. But the man of mediocre intelligence who is the professional mark-getter and who comes up to the Selective Process with a high standing in his class but with nothing else to offer, does not—according

87

to Dartmouth admissions concepts which I am not disposed to controvert—offer as much promise of contribution either as an undergraduate or ultimately as a citizen as the man whose intellectual equipment may be assumed to be approximately equal but who, having channeled his energies over a somewhat broader area, may present somewhat fewer A's.

When I undertook this work, I had a sub-conscious fear, which I did not recognize at the time, that a Selective Process which aimed for the "all-round man" was in grave danger of ending up with the mediocre. It was only after that fear had been substantially relieved by experience that I realized I had had it. Discerning school-men helped me over this hurdle, particularly in their evaluation of "mark-getters." Time after time we would find them saying, as one widely respected educator put it: "This boy would be a more liberally educated person if he were less self-centered and less concerned about his grades."

So when it is asked whether Dartmouth is now interested only in grades, the answer can be given with conviction that this is no more true than it ever was.

There is a reverse side to this coin. There is apparently a segment of the population which thinks that Dartmouth is a haven for lame ducks. A disappointed mother said to me last spring, more in sorrow than in anger: "I thought Dartmouth, of all places, would understand Tommy's low marks." A New Jersey man came in with his two sons. The older one's academic credentials were very dubious and I was unable to be very encouraging. After that situation had been covered, I turned to the younger lad with the doubtless fatuous conversational gambit: "Well, I suppose I'll be hearing from you one of these days." The father quickly interrupted: "No, Dickie gets very good grades and he thinks he wants to go to ———," and with a charming blush promptly bit off his tongue.

Actually, of course, Dartmouth is not, compared to its sister institutions, either an asylum for lame-brains, a Mecca for "greasy grinds," or a closed congregation of cerebral Colossi. It is true, of course, that some of the men whom we admit have been, or will be, turned down by our sister institutions, while every year some of those to whom we have said "no" turn up on these same campuses. This sort of thing can happen by the "rub of the green." But, in spite of ostensible differences in admissions systems, the type of candidates sought and the competitive situation which they face, are undoubtedly very similar in this group of colleges and universities.

A word of warning is perhaps in order to the "mark-getter's" antithesis, the "activity boy," who rushes around involving himself in a multitude of clubs, organizations, and activities without achieving real distinction in any of them or in scholarship either. These assiduous dilettantes and busybodies must be assessed a notch below the professional "mark-getter," who at least knows enough to put first things first and avoid spreading himself too thin.

We sometimes find a candidate apologizing for the fact that he is not a varsity athlete. This is ridiculous. Sometimes we find alumni sponsors professing to apologize for the fact that their protégés are accomplished in sports. This is equally silly, or insincere, or both. Men who have real distinction in athletics and sportsmanship have a valuable contribution to make to undergraduate life. So do men who have real distinction in music, dramatics, debating, journalism, and in other special skills and pursuits, and whose qualities of leadership have won notable recognition from their contemporaries. And if they are *outstanding* in any of these qualifications, it is important that we know it, as it is often difficult to distinguish the merely average or superior from the superlative.

After all this has been said, it must be re-emphasized that scholarship remains the primary qualification. It would be gratuitous to remind an alumni audience that Dartmouth is an educational institution, not a boys' finishing school or an athletic association. It would be insulting to the *Alumni Magazine*'s readers to belabor this point, but since an occasional correspondent enjoins us "not to forget the average boy," the point perhaps should not be ignored altogether.

It is well known that all the professional schools screen their men primarily on scholarship, whether for law, medicine, engineering, or teaching. And there is every tendency for business to do the same. The libraries are full of reference material on this point. The piece which I happen to have at hand, recently recalled to my attention by a friend, is an article appearing in *Harper's Magazine* some years ago entitled "Does Business Want Scholars?" by Walter S. Gifford. This article is largely based on a study of the Bell System by Dartmouth's eminent E. K. Hall '92.

The answer that Mr. Gifford gives to his own question is of course an emphatic "yes." He quotes an earlier study by President Foster of Reed College with a similar interrogatory title, "Should Students Study?", in which the conclusion is reached: "Indeed it is likely that the first quarter in scholarship of any school or college class will give to the world as many distinguished men as the other three-quarters."

Mr. Gifford—after carefully recognizing that salary and success are not necessarily synonymous, but assuming that in business they largely parallel each other, and granting that there are occasional notable exceptions—shows that in the Bell System men from the middle third of their college classes do better salary-wise than men from the last third, that the difference is still greater between men from the first third and men from the middle third, and that a still greater differential exists between those from the first tenth and the rest of the first third, and that the differentials between these four groups *increase with every passing year.*

Each of us can point out, as some have pointed out to me, individuals who barely squeaked through college, or flunked out of college, or didn't go to college at all, but who have had the most distinguished of careers. These are men who did not get their superior intelligences organized or motivated until later. But surely no one will argue that they achieved their successes because of, rather than in spite of, their deficiencies in scholarship.

The writer of this piece and most of its readers are average men. Most of us can find in our lives sufficient sources of satisfaction and self-respect. But we do not derive these satisfactions from our averageness. Those mornings when we feel especially good we do not walk down the street throwing out our chests and saying, "Gee, it's wonderful to be mediocre!" No more can we propose that a

8. President John Sloan Dickey matriculating the Class of 1951 in September, 1947. Director of Admissions Dickerson looks on. Below: Dickerson with Edward T. Chamberlain, Jr. 36, assistant director, in the fall of 1947.

college admissions office should set out in purposeful pursuit of mediocrity. The averages will take care of themselves.

Perhaps President Dickey had some of these factors in mind in his magnificent talk to the Alumni Council last June, when he spoke of the danger that alumni bodies might seek to "cast their colleges in their own molds." He was not speaking particularly of Dartmouth in this connection, but we Dartmouth men, who play a uniquely active and vital and influential part in the life of our college, cannot ignore the injunction.

There is one type of average boy who is all but irresistible. We have all seen these and few of us have been able to resist their appeal: the boys with exceptionally engaging personalities and boundless Dartmouth enthusiasm whom, for convenience, I shall call—with genuine friendliness and no contempt—"personality boys." I remember one such who was sent to me by a friend a year or so ago. I went overboard for him and sent my testimonial to the admissions office, to join with all the others, concerning "the most engaging average boy I ever saw." He was admitted and, out of curiosity, I looked into his record the other day. It was bulging with obviously genuine evidences of strong Dartmouth ambitions since infancy. But unhappily, he was then on the brink of flunking out, and it was evident that if he should survive by the skin of his teeth, it would be with a minimum contribution to Dartmouth's intellectual or community life. Personality and Dartmouth enthusiasm are just not enough.

After considering (1) the mind, (2) drive, vigor, determination, etc., (3) geographical distribution, and (4) general diversification, we have invaded a number of byways in discussing (5) diversity of interest in the individual man. Finished, at last, with interpretation of the principles of the Selective Process, we can sketch out its procedures before turning to alumni sons.

PROCEDURES OF SELECTION

Application for admission to Dartmouth may be made for a candidate anytime between the "It's a boy!" flash and March 1 of the boy's last year in secondary school—and preferably at least a few months before the latter deadline. All that is required is a small preliminary application card—no fee.

In the fall of the senior secondary-school year, we ask all those so registered with us if they are still interested. To those who say "yes" we send, during the late fall, three application forms and instructions. Form 1, to be filled out by the candidate, asks for full personal and biographical details. Form 2 asks the candidate to pen, without help, a handwritten letter to the director of admissions, telling about his special interests, the factors that have contributed to his development, and his expectations of college in general and Dartmouth in particular.

Form 3 is the "Personal Rating by Alumnus," which is to be handed by the candidate to someone who knows him well and who will complete the form and send it directly to us. An alumnus is suggested because he knows both the College and the candidate. But if the candidate has not been well acquainted for some time with a Dartmouth man, he should give the form to someone who does know him well. This person is expected to be prejudiced in favor of the candidate, but he will not serve the candidate well by writing him up as a Messiah when the rest of his papers will indicate that he is substantially less than that.

Before the Christmas holidays, we start channelling the Form 6's through the Alumni Councilors to the alumni interviewing committees across the country. We like to have the candidate interviewed, if possible, in his home community. These committees, although they will ask the applicant about his scholastic standing to make an over-all estimate of his promise, report chiefly on his personal qualities. These reports, more than anything else except possibly the candidate's letter, round out the picture of him as a human being and bring alive his folder-full of papers.

In late February, after the first half-year is completed in the schools, we start sending Forms 4 & 5 to the school principals. On Form 4, the principal evaluates the applicant's seriousness of purpose, industry, initiative, influence, concern for others, emotional stability, etc., and writes an informal supplementary paragraph describing what kind of person and student the applicant is. On Form 5, he gives the applicant's complete school record in detail, his standing in class, his strong and weak subjects, the results of tests he has taken, and an opinion with regards to the applicant's comparative promise as a prospect for admission to Dartmouth. These are the key documents in the Selective Process, based as it is on what the candidate has demonstrated that he not only can but *will* do. The school men are extraordinarily painstaking, discriminating, and honest in their evaluations; and they realize, of course, that their schools are rated by us on the degree to which their graduates live up to these predictions.

Only rarely do we find a school man trying to sell us one of his fourth-rate seniors, and from these infrequent instances we get some of the all-too-few laughs that there are in this business. These write-ups, without too much exaggeration, run something like this: "Dear Sir:

"I can give Blob Doolittle my warmest recommendation for admission to Dartmouth. It is true that he is in the lower ranges of the fourth quartile (259 in 260), but as you know, Hilltop Academy's selection is so careful, and our standards of grading and promotion so severe, that there is actually no such thing as a second, third, or fourth quarter at Hilltop. Actually, Blob only began to show his true intellectual power at the grading period week before last, when he almost got up to the college certifying level in two of his four courses. Our passing mark is 50, and we set our college certifying level at 35. Our honors mark is 38, high honors at 40, and highest honors at 41½. Ordinarily, fewer than 99% of a class achieves highest honors, but in this year's extraordinarily able senior class all members came through with flying colors. Blob, although a little shy in his marks, qualified by winning some extra points through his loyal service as Assistant Captain of the Mimeograph Squad. He has had some difficulty meeting Hilltop standards in English, mathematics, history and the foreign languages, but he is now beginning to show real strength in all of them and will certainly do at least average work at Dartmouth. Personally, Blob Doolittle is a boy of charming personality, cultured family, and fine character and integrity.

"In fairness to Blob, perhaps I should put in proper perspective that adolescent escapade of his sophomore year in which he attacked his house mother with a hand grenade, tommy gun, and machete. Mrs. Carmichael was such a beloved character on the campus before her unfortunate demise that we could hardly overlook the incident, and we had to suspend him for 48 hours. He won the heart of every member of the Disciplinary Committee by the way he took his punishment like a man. Things took a somewhat more serious turn last week when Blob was unfortunately discovered smoking corn-silks behind the gymnasium by the janitor's blind mother-in-law, after hours. For this grave infraction of discipline, we are having to withhold his diploma, and I hope it will not prejudice his chances at Dartmouth. I think the Trustees may grant him the coveted Hilltop sheepskin at a special meeting next week.

"Blob has real athletic promise, having been alternate on his house volleyball team during the summer term of 1943 (when he was taking his French and algebra for the third time). Any college which enrolls this fine young man will be fortunate. He would add tone to any group."

As a candidate's several forms come in they are separately read, evaluated, appropriately underlined and annotated, and rated. These ratings, along with a good deal of summarized information, are put on a master card for every candidate which, when completed, gives a quite comprehensive picture of the candidate.

In late March, when the bulk of the applications are complete, they are piled (master-cards attached) mountainously around a barricaded room. Each folder is then read as a whole. Those clearly superior are marked tentatively for admission. Those obviously inferior are marked for non-acceptance. When, after a couple of morning-to-midnight weeks of work, this process is completed, there remains a substantial group of applications which have been set aside. These are then examined again, with particular attention to such things as weak spots in English, mathematics, or the foreign languages, and repeated courses in which grades have to be discounted. By this time, the critical competitive level for the class has been determined and, measuring the individual applications against this yardstick, the final selections are made.

I was, I confess, a little surprised and no little relieved to find that this critical level is determinable with fair precision, as I had feared that there might be elements of whim or lottery in the final stages of narrowing down the marginal group. It was a comfort after it was all over to feel, without assuming infallibility, that reasonably precise and punctilious justice had been done.

Candidates who expect to increase their chances of selection by coming to Hanover for an interview should not be encouraged to incur such expense unless they are personally eager to visit the college and discuss their problems. We are delighted to see and talk to them; but, drawing as we do from a nation-wide, and to some degree world-wide, constituency, we could never expect to see more than a fraction of them personally (even though the director and assistant director are now spending at least 75% of their time during office hours on such interviews); and in these circumstances, weight cannot be given to these interviews in selection. Our alumni interviewing system is an admirable substitute.

As for a multitude of "recommendations," one well-known admissions director declares that his selections are made by hefting all the folders and throwing away the heaviest ones. There is more than a little validity to that procedure. When letters from friends-of-friends begin pouring in from all over about a candidate, you can't help starting to wonder what's wrong with him. Two or three letters from persons who really know the candidate well are helpful; letters from friends of his father add nothing to our picture of the candidate.

The preferential status enjoyed by candidates, for geographical or other reasons, is useful to them only if they fall in the marginal group, where it will gain admission for them in preference to other candidates of equal qualifications. There are no "quotas," whether for states, cities, schools, or any other groups.

So much for a very fragmentary account of how the system works.

SONS OF ALUMNI

Now we come to the question of sons of alumni. I almost said "problem"—but that would be grossly unfair. This group is anything but a problem. Through the years of my association with the College, I have looked through the lists of class officers, of athletic teams and captains, of men of distinctive scholastic accomplishment, and have found a more than liberal sprinkling of names of sons of Dartmouth men, and I am sure that this group has contributed to the life of the College far out of proportion to its size. All our experience with Dartmouth sons leads us to expect more rather than less of them, and the College would be incalculably the poorer without their contribution to college life. Furthermore, there is an intangible thing of great significance to the spirit and tradition of the College in having these threads of family tradition run through successive generations—often many of them.

The problem in this connection arises with the sharp increase in the number of applications, the concomitant increase in the number of disappointments, and the effect of these on the morale of the alumni body. The size of Dartmouth classes just about doubled during a brief period of years in the early 20's. Now the sons of these classes are just beginning to come of college age in substantial numbers and the doubling of the number of alumni-son applications is now well along. This year there were 250 alumni-son applicants; eventually there will be 350, perhaps more. Now, just statistically, doubling the number of applicants means the doubling of disappointments, without going into the question at all of raising the criteria which must be applied to this group. These disappointments inevitably produce wide repercussions through the alumni body.

With the number of alumni-son applicants reaching such a large figure, one may well ask the question whether it would be a good thing or a bad thing to have a class composed of from one-third to one-half sons of alumni. I think this is a question which is arguable and I am not going to try to answer it. Such a situation would have both its assets and its liabilities. The question is, to some degree, hypothetical and is not the real one which we must face up to.

The real question that we all must face up to with honesty and courage is the question whether alumni-son candidates must be expected to approximate the going competition for admission. There is no question which I have thought more about during the past year than this one.

I can see only one possible answer—that alumni sons must very closely approximate the going competition. If we turn away clearly superior candidates in these substantial numbers in order to admit alumni sons of lesser qualifications, I cannot see how it could have any other effect than to launch a steady deterioration of the College's standards and an inbred quality in the College which would, in the long run, be disastrous—an inbreeding to weakness rather than to strength.

Moreover, we cannot maintain decent relationships with the schools if we pass by their top-quarter boys of fine all-round qualifications in order to pick up third-quarter alumni sons. The natural speculation of the headmasters and principals in that situation is whether we are running an educational institution or a Dartmouth Club, and this question has actually been presented pretty straight a couple of times. One schoolman wrote me in a mood of sympathy: "I understand your situation there at Dartmouth and I shall not encourage any boys to apply for Dartmouth who do not have Dartmouth connections." It is clear what would happen to the College if this impression got a wide and firm hold in the schools.

Painful as is the necessity of facing this problem, we have got to face it squarely. I can see only one possible answer: that the utmost point to which preference can go is to give admission to a preferred candidate over another candidate of approximately *equal* qualifications.

President Dodds of Princeton sent a letter to all Princeton alumni last April. The following paragraph is quoted to indicate the extent to which Princeton has likewise been facing up to questions of policy relating to applications from sons of Princeton men.

"The problems of the Committee on Admission would be simplified greatly if the University could admit every applicant with

Princeton affiliations without reference to the credentials of other applicants. But I know that very few Princeton alumni would countenance a policy which would cut us off progressively from the rest of America. Convinced, as we are, that Princeton provides a superior education for responsible citizenship, we should be unfaithful to our stewardship, unworthy of the confidence of alumni and others who have demonstrated their faith in Princeton, and remiss in our duty to the country if our qualifications for admission were not fair and equitable to all, and were not based in each case on capacity, attainment, character and personality as demonstrated in free and equal competition."

You will find some alumni who will argue seriously and apparently with honest conviction that every son of an alumnus ought to be given the opportunity to flunk out of Dartmouth. Obviously, from what I have said, I do not consider that defensible or even possible College policy. Not only can we not afford to admit men who are not pretty clearly able to carry college work at a minimum level, but we cannot in the long run afford to admit those who do not measure up to the prevailing competition. What happens otherwise was indicated in a recent meeting of the Committee on Administration when four out of five of the problem cases before the Committee were alumni sons.

I wonder whether those who argue for the flunking out privilege have considered this carefully from the point of view of the effect on the alumnus and on the son. An alumnus has just written me from Tacoma commenting on some of these questions. He says:

"A number of years ago I was talking to the father of a son who had been admitted to Dartmouth, but who was later separated because of scholastic difficulty. The father told me he felt that it would have been better if the boy had never been admitted. I think he felt that though it would have been a disappointment not to have been admitted, it would have been much better in the long run to have accepted that disappointment, rather than later being faced with the frustration of just not being able to make the grade. There was more danger of permanent frustration from the latter than from the former.

"When I was in San Francisco last May, I talked with a friend of mine who graduated from Yale, and in the course of the conversation, I mentioned that his boy would probably be going there soon. He remarked that the way things were nowadays, he didn't know whether the boy could get into Yale or not. So I guess other institutions are having their problems also."

Actually, of course—and this is almost impossible for an alumnus parent to recognize—after we consider each alumni-son candidate as an individual case (and heaven knows we do consider them at length and with care and prayer) we also have to consider them as a group. The alumnus whose son has been turned down almost invariably will argue that even if his boy has no better than a 50-50 chance to survive at Dartmouth, we can afford to gamble on him. If there were only one such alumni son, or even if there were only six or twelve, we might out of deference to a father's lifetime devotion and service to the College, accede to his request and make the gamble. But when you have more than one hundred of these candidates who, in relation to the prevailing competition, are submarginal (and this number will rapidly increase), you are gambling with stakes that are far too high for the College to afford.

This is in essence the alumni-son question and I am confident that the conclusions indicated fairly represent the position of the President and Trustees. The Alumni Council at its meeting last June considered this question. The Council's Committee on Admissions and Schools in its report commented: "Dartmouth has always been an alumni college, but the College has grown and changed since our day. Due to the increase in the number of applicants for admission to the College and to the greatly increased numbers of Dartmouth sons applying for admission, this committee feels that Dartmouth fathers and their sons must recognize that from here on the sons will have to meet keener competition for selection. The Selective Process, in other words, which has always given preference to Dartmouth sons, should continue to do so but the sons will have to meet the competition of that year, both in regard to academic and other factors of the process. We hope and believe that Dartmouth sons should always receive preference, other things being equal or nearly equal." The Council voted to approve the report of the Committee and "to endorse specifically the portions of the report dealing with the admission of Dartmouth sons."

From the alumni relations point of view, there is an educational job to be done among alumni parents. For example, one Saturday afternoon last December an alumnus telephoned me and asked if it were necessary for his boy, as the son of an alumnus, "to go through the motions of filling out these application forms that you have sent to him?" As it turned out, the boy was one of the most hopelessly unprepared among all the 6,000 applicants this year. When he was turned down, the father was quite shocked and very, very angry. Another alumnus wrote to say that he had two sons and to ask whether he should enter applications for them or whether they would automatically be admitted when they came of college age. Now this sort of thing must seem almost incredible to those of you who are closer to the College, but it obviously exists, and rather widely.

I hope alumni will continue to make their sons want to go to Dartmouth more than to any other place, but they must, at the same time, make the boys realize that getting into Dartmouth is a job they have to work at. As they approach college age, if their aptitude for college work seems in doubt, these parents must prepare themselves and prepare their sons for the fact that there are alternatives to a Dartmouth education.

In conclusion let me say that we have not yet got trouble enough. Even after these hectic months, I still hold with Browning, as I have twice said to the Alumni Council, that our reach should continue to exceed our grasp. We do not want, heaven knows, any more applications *per se,* but we do want and will always want *more of the best ones.* We cannot, as the maxim goes, stand still without going backward, and we cannot stop until all the best boys from all the schools throughout the country want to go to Dartmouth. This, of course, can never happen; but instead of selling out for our share of the best boys, we must always be out to get as much more than our share as we can possibly get.

9. As Director of Admissions, Al Dickerson speaks to men of the Class of 1952 at Moosilauke Ravine Lodge during the Freshman Trip in September 1948.

Letter to an Alumnus

July 18, 1958

Dear Bill:*

Some time ago Tim Traquair sent me a copy of a letter from you to him concerning your contribution to the Capital Gifts Campaign and raising some questions about the College's policies on admission. During this period of the late spring I have to deal simultaneously with two freshman classes—the present one in the throes of winding up its freshman year and the incoming one with its variety of questions about courses, rooms and one thing and another looking to the opening of College in the fall. So, hoping to make thoughtful comments on the questions you discuss, I have several times started and then postponed writing to you during these rather hectic days.

I have thought quite a good deal about the questions that you raise. It is quite a common thing for Dartmouth men of our generation to ask these days: "Would I be admitted if I applied today?", and the answer has to be given that probably quite a few of us wouldn't. I think of individual men in our generation, including some classmates of ours, who—judging from what they tell me about their high school and prep school records—probably wouldn't get into Dartmouth today and I think of what the College would have lost if they hadn't been Dartmouth men—of what they contributed to our mutual experience as undergraduates, of their effectiveness as workers in various Dartmouth causes, of the respect that they have won for Dartmouth as representatives of the College in

---

*William O. Lucas '30.

their individual lives, their service to their communities, their positions in business and the professions. Approaching this question thus, on an ad hominem basis, looking through the eyes of a friend on Classmate X and Classmate Y and Alumnus Z, one can hardly come away from such reflections without the feeling that Dartmouth would be irreparably the poorer if they were not Dartmouth men. And maybe it would.

Perhaps this is as good a place in this letter as any other to say that the answers to the questions which your letter raises, both directly and by implication, have not yet been written. It may be that these answers may not be written with any assurance or finality for a good long time, because the frontiers of human measurement and prediction are still challenging and baffling science. But at any rate, a new effort to arrive at the best possible answers for Dartmouth's foreseeable future is going to be launched this fall by the Trustees Planning Committee, which within the past fortnight has scheduled for this fall the establishment of a subcommittee to examine the area of admission and the very closely related area of financial aid.

You very likely know about the work of the Trustees Planning Committee, which has been created by the Trustees to do long-range planning looking forward to the bicentennial in 1969. Its assignment is to plan for all areas of Dartmouth life. As studies are completed, recommendations are turned over to the Trustees and other agencies for realization. The aim is "to get a running start on Dartmouth's third century"; to arrive at the bicentennial date not merely with a high flown collection of aspirations, but with the maximum amount of *achieved excellence* in all areas of college life. The Capital Gifts Campaign is, of course, part of this program aimed at pre-eminence for Dartmouth College on all fronts.

The TPC subcommittee on admissions and financial aid has not yet been appointed, but if you want to send me any further thoughts on admissions policies I will see that these are transmitted to the committee for consideration.

Now, leaving the future of admissions policies for later determination, let me try to give you some comments on your questions based on my experience in Dartmouth admissions in the post-war decade. I learned about admissions the hard way, being plunged into it suddenly on Bob Strong's death in 1946, during which year applications were abruptly tripled over my previous experience. We have a similar multiplication of applications in prospect between now and 1970, during which period the college-age population will be doubled.

You mention the possibility of increasing Dartmouth's size. I have come somewhat reluctantly to the conclusion that this is desirable, within limits; and in fact, TPC planning is being done on the assumption of a 25% increase, from 2600 to 3000, on which we've gone more than half-way already. But even if we doubled or tripled Dartmouth's size—which no one has suggested—we couldn't make any real dent on the national problem.

So we start consideration of the admissions problem with X number of places and Y number (larger than X) of applicants. Whatever the relative size of the two figures, the problem is essentially the same: what criteria are you going to use in selecting the ones to be admitted? What kinds of excellence are we seeking in our students?

Let me indicate some of the assumptions which I would make and which I believe you would make, too:

1. That the first quality an educational institution must expect in its students is educability: i.e., good minds and an interest in learning.
2. That the two prime elements of greatness in any college are (a) its faculty and (b) its student body.
3. That each of these is equally important and equally dependent on the other; i.e., you can't attract a first-rate student body with a second-rate faculty and you can't maintain a first-rate faculty if you give them second-rate students. In this assumption I am assuming that *one* essential criterion of excellence in a student—but by no means the only one—is educability.

So then, if you are faced with the necessity—and opportunity—of selecting X number of students from Y number of applicants, what criteria beyond (a) a good mind and (b) a desire to learn, will you apply in selecting your students?

I think we will agree that we should look for good character, human decency, integrity—to the extent that these qualities can be identified and measured.

Beyond these qualities, I think we may properly look for a diversity of talents—not necessarily in the individual student, but in the student body. In Dartmouth admissions we have shied away from the cliche of "well-roundedness," which tends to mediocrity. We don't expect each student to be good at everything. But ideally we would like every one to be very good at some one thing besides studies—whether it be music, athletics, conchology, or whatever. Not all of them are, of course. But I for one regard this as a desirable goal for a college—to have each student bring with him some well-developed talent, and to have in the student body the maximum diversity not only of personal interests and abilities but also of economic, social, and geographic background.

Any arguments so far, Bill? Actually, these have been the stated goals of Dartmouth's admissions since we pioneered with the Dartmouth Selective Process in 1921.

I suspect what concerns you is what also sometimes concerns me. I am thinking of a particular classmate of ours whom I like very much, and who has done a lot for Dartmouth and our class. He wasn't a strong student, took an extra year in prep school, etc., and maybe we would be accurate in guessing that he wouldn't be admitted today. Will the man who fills X's place in the Class of 1963, because he has higher grades and better College Board aptitude scores, also bring to Dartmouth the fine qualities of our classmate X—loyalty, enthusiasm, solidity, capacity for friendship, unselfishness, readiness to serve? This is, I think, the most important question of college admissions. I personally believe that the answer is "yes"—that the class of '63 and '73, if we select them well, can bring to Dartmouth not only a higher average educability but also the respectworthy personal qualities that you and I admire in our Dartmouth friends X, Y and Z.

I think the key word in your letter is not "average," but rather is "democracy." I don't believe that you and I, who want Dartmouth to be excellent in every respect, would want to qualify that to the extent of saying we want Dartmouth to excel in everything else but have only an "average" quality of student body, assuming we could define "average" for this purpose. My guess is that you wouldn't want to have Dartmouth lose any of the diversity of, say, that interesting group of characters who started out with us in Hubbard Hall in the fall of 1926. And I wouldn't either.

There are lots of debatable questions about just which kinds of excellence we should seek in our students in the future, as admission becomes increasingly competitive. I'd be interested, as I said earlier, in what qualities you would have Dartmouth look for. I believe anyone who knows American colleges well would put Dartmouth among, say, the top dozen colleges in quality of student body—whatever different criteria different judges might employ. You mention Harvard. Harvard has a distinct edge on Dartmouth in terms of the *average* educability of its entering classes; and the recent issues of the annual reports from Harvard's Committee on Admission reflect concern regarding excessive homogeneity among entering classes of increasingly high academic aptitude and motivation. But leaving Harvard aside, on the educability criterion we have to yield at present to Princeton, too, and Yale and Amherst among, probably, others, with respect to the quality of educability as measured by average aptitude test scores and rank in secondary school class.

Whatever may be decided upon as the qualities Dartmouth should seek in its candidates of the future, I for one hope that by 1969 we will be the *best*—if not before. And my guess is that you agree.

Tell me more about your boy and his record. I don't think that in your day or mine we will see Dartmouth classes filled with such paragons as your letter describes. The preferential consideration for sons of alumni continues to apply—up to the point where neither you nor I would want to put a son of ours into a competition in which the odds would be too heavily against his success and survival.

All the best to you, Bill.

Sincerely,
Al Dickerson

A True Dog Story*

In which Amherst squirrels and Dartmouth dogs
  vie for numerical honors, and an allergic
applicant for '57 gets a free and bewildering
  correspondence course in the liberal arts

As a journal devoted to letting Dartmouth men know what goes on in Hanover, we hate to admit this, but it was not until we had read the October issue of the *Amherst Alumni News* that we knew anything at all about an epistolary imbroglio involving Amherst, Dartmouth, their respective directors of admissions, an unaccommodated applicant for college, dogs, squirrels, acorns, and hundreds and hundreds of words.

Knowing that the mere mention of Hanover dogs will immediately arouse the most intense sort of interest on the part of Dartmouth men, we hasten to fill in what Albert I. Dickerson '30, Dartmouth's erudite director of admissions, would call a lacuna in our coverage of College affairs.

The whole business began when Dean Eugene S. Wilson of Amherst received a most unusual inquiry from a young applicant in the East:

Dear Sir:

I should like to enter Amherst College, Fall, '53. On that hope I am writing for a catalogue.

However, a condition may preclude my application. I am allergic to dogs, their antics, and their barking. Their actual presence itself

*From the December 1953 issue of the *Dartmouth Alumni Magazine*

does not disturb me—not the dogs themselves—only their activities.

Should Amherst, the community, be hospitable to dogs, then Amherst College would not be for me. A university in a large city would afford me a desirable condition on the dog problem. But—should your judgment conclude that I might not be comfortable at Amherst, just ignore my request for a catalogue.

Yours sincerely,
William B. Rogers.

Having on previous occasions had his leg pulled by his Dartmouth counterpart, Dean Wilson for a number of reasons suspected a repeat performance and replied as follows:

My dear Mr. Rogers:

Amherst is a small community and, like all small country communities, very fond of dogs. The town is full of them—they even invade the dormitories and classrooms. They are, for the most part, well-mannered dogs and dogs of unusual breeding. But this does not interest you, a person who is allergic to them.

In the heart of our campus is an oak grove, and these oaks bear many acorns. All year long squirrels engage themselves in burying these acorns. Many of the dogs in the town know about these squirrels and spend hours stalking them from one corner to another. That is why we have so many dogs on the Amherst campus.

Have you thought of Dartmouth College, a very fine institution north of Amherst? So far north, it is too cold for dogs. I suggest you investigate this institution as well as city institutions.

You may have heard some rumors about there being a good many old dogs in Hanover, but on scientific exploration we found, through our Smith College agents, that these old dogs are wolves of the two-legged variety. Though they are playful, they are not dangerous. In our state there is an open season on them at all times with no bag limit. They are such easy hunting that few people bother to chase them any more. As our local haberdasher said last week: "I took three of them for plenty a week ago Saturday, but it was so easy that I hesitated to speak about it."

If you do write Dartmouth, address your letter to Mr. A. I. Dickerson, their director of admission. He will be sympathetic with your allergy problem because he is allergic to many things, but dogs is not one of them.

> Sincerely,
> Eugene S. Wilson,
> Director of Admission

The story next takes on a certain piquancy with the development that Mr. Dickerson was innocent, this time, and that Mr. Rogers apparently was no figment of the imagination. The young gentleman was quickly heard from again:

Dear Dr. Wilson:

I take my pen in hand to indite to you a reply to your reply to an inquiry of mine as to the state of the dog cult upon the Amherst campus.

The job is not an easy one for a single reason: I can't quite make you out as you reveal yourself in your epistle on this item of social interest.

Are you a philosophical character—a psychological structure—concerned with getting something said which will not let itself be put in phraseology understandable to the commonalty—to such who have not a college degree, but are determined to acquire one, hoping in the process to gain what is the crux of the matter, some information, some inspiration, of course, some amusement?

Should I make up my mind to matriculate at Amherst College, in spite of the dogs, vying with the squirrels in burying acorns in one corner or the other of the campus—and be accepted (more of the condition)—I would closely study you.

Of Dartmouth I have never heard. On second thought, a guy from this place is said to be playing football at a school bearing that name, a few steps nearer the Pole than Amherst. But, never having heard of the Dartmouth joint, before this "personal" showed up in the public prints, I choose to persist in my lifelong conditioning, negatively, to the effect that there is no such place as Dartmouth!

That Smith College? I know ten thousand Smiths, but that there is a Smith College—I say, quit your kidding. However, giving to the idea a thorough going over, I am willing to take your statement at face value and consider this Smith school an institution where some FBI's are trained—you write darkly of "your Smith College agents."

But truly, your paragraph about the dogs of Dartmouth who are actually wolves, but playful wolves, the sort of animal that in your state may be bagged by the gunful quite legally, and open-mindedly, haberdashers doing so without guns, has me topsy turvy.

Really, what I gather from the brambles of your letter is, I am not wanted at Amherst College. That's that. Very well. So!

But why did you not do as I suggested—that, in case you were not the place for me, you would ignore my letter about my coming?

And why suggest I write to this fellow—A. I. Dickerson—evidently a dog worshipper—about Dartmouth? Oh, why!

Oh, why! Let me tell you—to be nasty. Dog worshippers *hate* non-dog worshippers!

With an In Faith, Hope and Charity.

Yours sincerely,
William B. Rogers

Enclosed with this letter was a communication from another eastern college advising him, in all frankness, that "it would not be wise for me to encourage you to matriculate here," and wishing him every success in "the planning of your future education."

Mr. Dickerson, apprised of what was afoot at Amherst and of the suspicion that had been directed his way, now enters the epistolary lists. As a warm-up he wrote Dean Wilson's secretary a letter which we quote in part:

Yours of the 19th inst. opened. "Mr. Wilson has gone out of town again." I hope you will make a note of that for his epitaph.

By the way, while you are working on Mr. Wilson's epitaph, you might make a note of Mr. Rogers' concluding words: "Just ignore my request for a catalogue." It strikes me that when Mr. Wilson is firmly planted under Amherst's sod, Mr. Rogers might well have contributed the headline for the Wilson gravestone. . . .

> Sincerely,
> A. I. Dickerson

P.S. As I am leaving on a trip to Cleveland before this letter is transcribed, I am asking my secretary to sign and send it in my absence.

"On the same day," states the *Amherst Alumni News*, "Dean Wilson determined the truth of Mr. Rogers' existence. 'As he was leaving town on a short trip,' he asked his secretary to forward the evidence to Mr. Dickerson 'and to say that he guesses there is really a guy who hates dogs.' He added his apologies for suspecting his Hanover colleague."

The prolix Mr. Dickerson, now thoroughly warmed up, spurred his dictating machine into a gallop, lowered his lance, and showed that he was just as scintillatingly adroit as he was in the days when he wrote "The Gilded Shovel" for *The Dartmouth* and the 1930 class notes for this magazine. By means of a carbon copy Dean Wilson was spared any lacuna in his knowledge of what Mr. Dickerson wrote to Mr. Rogers:

Dear Mr. Rogers:

Mr. Eugene Wilson, who is a very considerate person and, incidentally, one of rare charm, has thoughtfully sent to me his correspondence with you, so that I might have this background when I heard from you. Modest as Mr. Wilson is by instinct, I can see how he might have taken it for granted that you would be influenced by his eloquent representation on behalf of Dartmouth. Also, he knows how much I value every opportunity to enjoy the orotund, if sometimes obfuscated, quality of his prose.

Although it now appears clear that you could hardly be interested in either Amherst or Dartmouth as a college for yourself, I hope you will pardon me for thus thrusting myself gratuitously into this correspondence, in order to fill certain lacunae in it with regard to Amherst, Dartmouth, Smith, dogs, squirrels, and Mr. Wilson.

Perhaps we should take Dartmouth first, to clear away an air of unreality which seems to pervade this correspondence. Indeed, I am often troubled by the skepticism of this age. You question the very existence of Dartmouth College, one of America's most ancient institutions of higher learning, and one which is widely believed to be the liveliest intellectual center north of Chicopee; and you also throw into question the reality of Smith College, a seminary for young ladies which was founded by the Smith Brothers' sister, Sophia (who was one of the most famous beardless ladies of her time), and which is palpably and tremulously real. And I seem to detect, even in Mr. Wilson, himself, a certain skepticism about the essential reality of a Mr. William Rogers, who is allergic to the antics of dogs. This is surprising, because Mr. Wilson is widely respected by his many friends and admirers as a person of deep faith and understanding in matters of the spirit. However, Mr. Wilson's one weakness, if it may be called that, is a certain prankish penchant, which sometimes causes him to create elaborate fictional situations for the bewilderment of his more innocent-minded friends. This harmless and, indeed, somewhat charming human quality of mendacity in Mr. Wilson quite naturally leads him into the error of discovering the same quality in others who are, in fact, quite innocent of guile. (I might add, parenthetically, that the only justification for the title of Doctor, with which you salute him, is an honorary M.D. bestowed upon him in recognition of his prowess in the field of mendacity in early middle age (circa 1897). As it turned out, this was before he reached the fullness of his powers. Mr. Wilson is a late bloomer.)

I wish that I could conscientiously persuade your interest in Dartmouth. Your letters seem to reflect some unusual potentialities —not only a pith of phrase, but a rare power of apperception. Take, for example, your comment to Mr. Wilson: "Really, what I gather from the brambles of your letter . . ." —there you illuminate in a flash one of the most fascinating paradoxes in the Wilson character, a certain piquant prickly quality in his personality. As with certain personalities on a more heroic scale, it may be difficult sometimes "to see the forest for the trees," so with Dr. Wilson, one may, on first encounter have difficulty in seeing the thicket for the thorns. But, believe me, Mr. Rogers, there is real warmth and true goodness behind that nettlesome façade.

However, I guess we will just have to face it: unless you can sublimate your allergy to the antics of dogs, Dartmouth is not for you. Actually, with his customary modesty and generosity in discussing Amherst in relation to other colleges, I am afraid that Dr. Wilson overstated both the canine abundance of Amherst and the dog-poverty of Dartmouth. Indeed, a theory is widely held among authoritative biologists and archaeologists that there was a distinct migration of Canis Familiaris in the late Pleistocene northward from the miasmal meadows and swamps of the middle Connecticut River Valley to the hill country of this area where, all climatologists agree, the legendary dry cold provides a more beneficent environment for both man and beast. At any rate, dogs are a prominent feature of the domestic, social, and educational environment here; and it is only fair to you to recognize very frankly that the domestic canine strain is rather an antic one. This is true both in the general and in the particular. Symbolic of the environment is the fact that a large Labrador retriever accompanies the president of the College everywhere he goes. This dog, known as Rusty, originally had an antic spirit at least average for his environment, but he has quieted down somewhat of late. It is locally believed that this may be due to Rusty's habit of spending his office hours quietly masticating and digesting correspondence retrieved from the president's waste basket, which would have a sobering effect on anyone. Prior to Rusty, another canine symbol of great prominence and of uncertain origin was the most popular campus figure of his time. His activities and achievements were copiously covered in the daily press. He attended all athletic contests, baying in victory and howling in defeat. (He is chiefly remembered as a howler.) He gave nightly serenades in the center of the campus to the accompaniment of the College chimes, concerning which he had strong feelings. His most characteristic addition was to empty beer cans, with which he was plentifully supplied by visiting Amherst students. Indeed, one theory advanced at the time of his mysterious disappearance—although it must be said that there is no real evidence in support of it—was that he wandered off down the valley (in spite of the climatic and other advantages of this area) in quest of an even more abundant supply of beer cans, closer to the source. He had real élan with a beer can.

And so it goes. Dogs here go to class, to the library, to the movies, to the dining halls, and to church. On the playing fields, they usually outnumber the biped population by approximately two and one-half times, per square foot. The squirrel population is far, far behind. Out of courtesy to Mr. Wilson, I think I will drop the squirrel question right here. He is understandably somewhat confused about the ecological relationships of oaks, acorns, dogs, and squirrels: bionomics is not really Mr. Wilson's field.

Although your particular requirements, Mr. Rogers, seem to rule out Dartmouth for you, I do not feel that you should lightly dismiss the opportunities at Amherst, which are extraordinary in many respects. I happen to have an Amherst catalogue at hand and I am sending it to you. (I got this catalogue for my daughters because there is more information about Smith and Mount Holyoke in it than is available in their own publications.) You, yourself, have already recognized the instructive possibilities of studying Dr. Wilson. Amherst has many other advantages. It has a nice little library and unquestionably the best gymnasium in the whole Amherst, Smith, Mount Holyoke community, where books, musicians, psychiatrists, and shower rooms are so generously shared. In addition, there is a certain charm about the Amherst campus. Smith girls, for example, think that it is cute. I beg you, therefore, Mr. Rogers, not to summarily dismiss Amherst from your consideration simply because Mr. (I mean Dr.) Wilson quite pardonably let himself get just a little boastful about Amherst's dogs, squirrels, and acorns. If I can be of any further help to you with regard to your educational plans, please do not hesitate to get in touch with me.

Sincerely,
Albert I. Dickerson

Except for a few newspaper clippings about squirrels thoughtfully forwarded to Dean Wilson by Mr. Dickerson, l'affaire Rogers became a closed matter. "Where Mr. Rogers matriculated is unknown," concludes the Amherst magazine. "Certain it is, however, that he has been exposed to a liberal education." And exposed also, we would add, to the fact that directors of admissions are human enough to be frolicsome—even squirrelish—now and then.

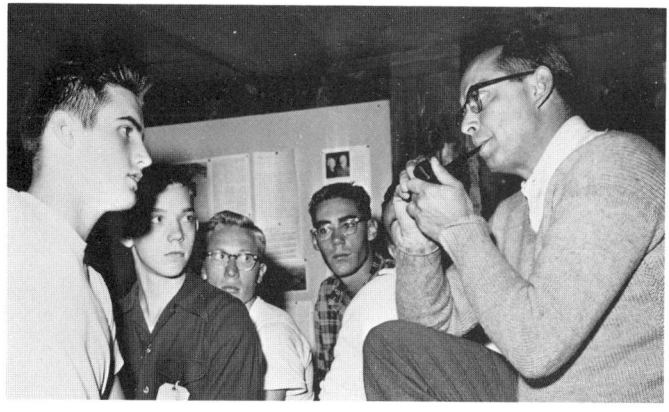

10. Al Dickerson, named chairman of the Committee on Scholarships and Loans in June 1952, in addition to his admissions post, shown on the steps of Parkhurst Hall with Robert K. Hage '35 (center), assistant director of admissions and executive secretary of the Financial Aid Office, and Donald W. Cameron '35, head of the new Office of Placement and Staff Personnel. Below: Dickerson, named Dean of Freshmen in 1956, meets with some of his charges that fall during the Freshman Trip.

11. *A 1961 photograph of Dean Dickerson in his Parkhurst Hall office.*

5. Dean of Freshmen

Mr. Dickerson was named Dean of Freshmen at Dartmouth College in 1956, and filled that position for sixteen years, until his death.

Mr. Dickerson's introduction of Robert Frost, who spoke to the freshman class in the fall of 1961.

MEN OF 1965:

I speak for your president, Mr. Frederick, and I know for each of you in acknowledging gratefully here this afternoon a unique moment in Dartmouth history. Many Dartmouth senior classes have sat here in this room with Mr. Frost in his yearly meetings in Great Issues. No previous freshman class has had this experience here or anywhere. I don't really know why this moment has been this long postponed, because, while Mr. Frost was once a Dartmouth freshman, he has never been a Dartmouth senior. By this time in his freshman year 70 years ago, he had shaken from his feet the dust of Hanover—or its snow or slush—and was teaching school in Massachusetts. He has been teaching ever since. He said yesterday that he had taught at every level except kindergarten. Today the world is his classroom and his province encompasses vast reaches of mystery and wonder beyond. I don't know what Mr. Frost will say or read to you today. He is consummately subversive. He takes a rather dim view of the machinery of education and, incidentally, of deans. Yet I doubt that he will advocate departure from college as the ineluctable path to greatness, even though it was his path. He was introduced yesterday when the Robert Frost Room was dedicated in the Library as "Dartmouth's most beloved son," and indeed he is. When his turn came, among his remarks he dropped the comment: "This is my college, you might say—the first college I ran away from." He also said, "It was here that I got my first impulse to publish," or, as he put it later, "to go into the poetry business."

Mr. Frost belongs to all colleges and to everybody, and we do not seek here to stake out Dartmouth's peculiar claims whether as the first or the best college he ever ran away from. But it is exciting to think of this as the 70th anniversary of Robert Frost's decision "to go into the poetry business."

You will see from the lights and the cameras that a few moments of this unique and intimate occasion are being shared with the world. I know you will not begrudge this.

Mr. Frost . . .

Meeting of the freshman class,
September 16, 1971, during Freshman Week
preceding the opening of college.

MR. DICKERSON:

Thank you, gentlemen, and good evening. "There are few earthly things more beautiful than a university," wrote John Masefield, one-time England's poet laureate, speaking in a context that fully encompasses this institution, though called a college. "It is a place" he continued, "where those who hate ignorance may strive to know, where those who perceive truth may strive to make others see, where seekers and learners alike banded together in the search for knowledge will honor thought in all its finer ways. It gives to the young in their impressionable years the bond of a lofty purpose shared, of a great corporate line whose links will not be loosed until they die. It gives young people that close companionship for which youth longs and that chance of the endless discussion of themes which are endless without which youth would seem a waste of time. There are few earthly things more splendid than a university. Wherever a university stands, it stands and shines. Wherever it exists, the free minds of men urged on to full and fair inquiry may still bring wisdom into human affairs."

We are gathered here tonight to welcome you into such an institution. And no one could more appropriately extend Dartmouth's welcome to you than the man who is primarily responsible for the fact that you are here rather than 820 other guys. Gentlemen, I give you your friend, the Director of Admissions, Mr. Chamberlain.

Another member of the platform group that is here just to stand up and be recognized is my associate, Dean Manuel, who, along with me will be sharing with you men the experience of your freshman year at Dartmouth. Mr. Manuel was a member of the Class of 1958 at Dartmouth. Among other things he had distinction as a baseball player; a record that he was fairly nifty with the bat and the glove. He tells me that he doesn't have a great arm and that's why he played first base. Anyway, subsequent to graduation he did a four-year tour of duty as a naval officer. Then he joined Mr. Chamberlain as Assistant Director of Admissions and for the past three years he's been at the University of Illinois doing graduate work toward a Ph.D. and, at the same time, I guess for a little food money, doing some counseling of Illinois students. I am very happy to have Dean Manuel with me. I am sure you will enjoy coming to know him between now and next June. Between us we hope to have met every one of you. We will start sending, in due course, little printed notes of invitation to invite you to come in and talk about your plans, your progress and your problems, if you have any, and if you get one of these little messages don't think you're in trouble. Just think that we would like to have a chat with you if you would like to have a chat with us. If you should be in trouble, we would have somewhat more urgent ways to communicate with you. But this we do not expect. We look forward to sharing with you the excitement of the freshman year, having satisfaction in all your successes, sharing any disappointments you may have during the course of the year, and between now and next June coming to count many of you as good friends.

Now, we are about to hear from our principal speaker this evening, the President of the College. Before introducing him, I do not have very much in the way of counsel to offer you. I am sure you will be disappointed. Mr. Chamberlain predicted that you'd be oversupplied with that commodity, and perhaps you will be, but I don't think you will be tonight. I recall during a period when I was in admissions work reading a statement from an applicant for admission who said, "I shall be ever grateful for the guidance and counsel inflicted upon me by my parents." I don't seek to earn that sort of gratitude from you. If I were to offer you one bit of advice it would be to try to organize your lives so that you get adequate sleep. I know from twelve years' experience in deaning freshmen that's a futile bit of counsel to offer and that you will stay up late and talk about late booking until you find out that it doesn't work and then you'll stop. I would encourage you to get involved in Dartmouth life. If you organize your time you will have time to do that; not to be just a spectator or a passive taker-in of what's going on around here. To get involved in something you'll need disciplining your time outside of your academic work, something that will take you outside of yourself, refresh your spirits and through which you may make contributions to the life of this community. I would encourage you to be a little bit scared as you start your freshman year because those who run scared run a little faster. I would urge you not to overdo it and, in this connection, I refer to one of the oldest jokes that I know which has always amused me, about people who go to the extreme of optimism and pessimism. There was a parent who had twin sons who were utterly identical in every respect except that one of them was a very extreme optimist and the other was a confirmed and despondent pessimist. The father asked a psychiatrist-friend of his what he might do to encourage these twin sons to make a more moderate approach in their estimate of life and the psychiatrist said, "Well, Christmas is coming. What do they want for Christmas?" The father said, "Well, the optimist is just dying for a pony—anything for a pony. The pessimist doesn't expect anything at all; hasn't indicated any desires because he doesn't really expect anything, but he did once mention that he could use a watch." So, the psychiatrist said, "Well, let's try just a little experience of shock. Get for your pessimist the finest 45-jewel platinum watch that can be bought. Put it in his stocking, and in the stocking of the optimist put some horse droppings; the optimist who wanted the pony." So the psychiatrist saw the boys a few days after Christmas and said, "Well, boys, how did Christmas go?" And the pessimist said, "Well, I got a watch. Don't think it will run very long. It's supposed to be solid platinum but I think it's plated.

That's the way it is." The psychiatrist turned to the optimist and said, "Well, how was your Christmas?" "Gee, great! I got a horse, but he got away." [Applause] So I suggest to you the middle way.

Office Memoranda

October 29, 1964

FROM: AID
TO: SP*
SUBJECT: Interviewing Techniques

I have given you orally the outline of my normal procedure for interviewing freshmen. This is not "the word," because I'm an amateur. I imagine by this time you have been able to have a conference with Hank Helgen to get his more skilled advice on interviewing techniques. I'd also like to have a session with Ray Sobel sometime on the question and maybe the two of us together could set up this; and if we do, possibly some of the other deans would like to join us.

Anyway, for better or for worse, let me give you my routines:

Usually I start off with a relaxed: "How are things going?"—to give the interview a routine complexion.

Then I usually go course by course to find how they are doing, who are their teachers, how they react to them, and how much time they are spending, per assignment, in studying for each course.

For the obviously highly successful student, I don't spend much time on study techniques. For the others—the majority—I usually ask how much time they spend studying, per assignment, where they study, how late they study, whether they have learned to use the daytime hour here and there between classes, etc. If they appear unorganized about study, I suggest working out a schedule and re-

*D. Scott Palmer '59, Assistant Dean of Freshmen, 1964 to 1969.

fer them to Bob Bear's course in reading and study techniques. I discourage late booking. If they appear to be unorganized studiers, I suggest they find some place congenial to them, where they do nothing but study—as against their desk where, with their girl's picture in front of them, they write letters and daydream. If they have serious problems of concentration, I refer them to Hank Helgen, as well as Bob Bear.

After covering courses and study habits, I usually ask about their prospective major and career goals. Unless they are doing very well in the most importantly relevant courses and know clearly what they want to do, I almost always suggest going to the Office of Student Counseling for a reading of the Strong Vocational Interest Inventories. I point out that these very seldom indicate any black-and-white choices and that they sometimes simply add further to the confusion in the student's mind, but that they are interesting and fun and frequently helpful.

I suggest that you go over to the Counseling Office to sit in on one of these sessions, if you haven't done so, so that you can describe to the freshmen what they are like and how they are handled.

If a man's reading scores are below the median, I suggest in a low pressure way that he might take advantage of Bob Bear's course on the grounds that all of us could profit by sharpening up our reading skills.

If the man has a set of high MMPI scores, I tend to prolong the conference to get a fuller reading on the boy.

I inquire about extracurricular activities without implying that a man should be in one. However, if in the admissions notes there are indications of talents in certain directions and I find that a man isn't pursuing them and it seems as though he could handle them, I frequently encourage him to pursue them.

Then the questions about roommates and dormitory conditions to get a picture of the student's social relationships.

If the cards indicate that the parents are divorced, I try—gently and without prying—to find out how long ago they were divorced and what are the relationships of the student with each of the two parents and with step-parents.

Whenever there is any reason to do so—distance, any indications of homesickness or other problems—I ask: "How are things at home?"—which includes, among other things, The Girl, and this sometimes brings out quite a lot.

Finally, and this is usually the most interesting and productive part of the interview, I open where appropriate with the gambit: "Well, you don't seem to have any problems." And then ask the question: "Have you got anything on your mind?"

Often, this is where the real interview begins.

Two 1972's whose group on their Freshman Trip bought red hats and wore them most of their freshman year paid calls on the Dean of Freshmen just before vacations throughout their years at Dartmouth and surprised him annually on his birthday with an afternoon bottle of champagne. On one of their pre-Christmas calls the Dean was conferring with a freshman in his "inner office." The two callers received at home the following:

DARTMOUTH COLLEGE
Disciplinary Report

December 11, 1969

Name	Class
Daniel S. Moors	1972
Gregory C. Yadley	1972

Date of Infraction: December 9, 1969

Time: circa 4:00 p.m.

Place: 102 Parkhurst Hall

Charge: Snowball assault on 102 Parkhurst Hall. Contumacious remarks to and about the Dean of Freshmen's receptionist.

Report: Disguised (i.e., *sans chapeaux rouges*), these men entered 102 Parkhurst Hall without prior assignment or advisement, attempted to enter the inner office but were barred by the Registrar of Freshmen and Freshman Receptionist from ingress. Egress completed voluntarily. Then assaulted outer windows with snowballs.

Disposition: Sorry I missed you. Glad you missed me. The snowballs come at $10 each. (Do not send check or money order.) Contumacious Conduct charges referred to UGC-JC, Hanover graveyard.

        Albert I. Dickerson
        Dean

January 12, 1971

FROM: Albert I. Dickerson
TO: Files
SUBJECT: The Vegetarianism of John Smith '74

This morning I became the 5th or 6th College officer with whom John Smith has consulted concerning this matter (Messrs. Rugg, Jackson, Moore, Brewster, etc.).

I went through the whole question of contract dining as the most effective way to provide good and economical institutional food, and again went through the fact that contract dining cannot work if administrative officers are loose with exceptions which cannot be defended in the face of varieties of applications from students wanting to be excused for often whimsical or capricious reasons. He granted all of this, and yet always wound up in the same place.

His first pitch is for Thayer Hall to offer him a special vegetarian diet. As an alternative, in the end, the only one that is satisfactory, is that he be excused from a DDA contract, although he claims he would like to eat there with his friends. He claims that he lost 25 pounds during the first term trying to live on a vegetarian diet in Thayer Hall, and since he is out for the squash team it's important for him to have an adequate diet. He says that his family just cannot afford to maintain a Thayer Hall contract to be supplemented from the Main Street establishments. I intimated that I did not really find this an unbearable financial burden.

His vegetarianism is based on "moral" not on "religious" reasons.

He saw no point in discussing the matter with Chaplain Rahmeier and I didn't push it.

I then suggested that we go to Thayer Hall for lunch on non-meat proteins. Going through the cold line and making a supplementary trip through the hot line, we did resoundingly well and John readily conceded that he would not be undernourished for his squash games this afternoon. Since John is currently ranking about 21st on the squash ladder, the squash problem doesn't strike me as a major one, but naturally he views it differently.

He complains that for breakfast the eggs run out regularly before the established end of the breakfast hour. I told him I would look into this with Mr. Moore, but if his eggs were that important he might well want to get up early enough to be sure that he got there before the supply ran out.

John's cause was a little bit deflated by the abundance and variety of proteins on his plate. I suspect the matter will not end here. He suggested that he might ask his personal physician, Dr. Burnett, to write a note to Dr. Jackson. I did not discourage this. I also told him that I'd be glad to discuss the matter with his parents, whom I know well, especially if they viewed this as an intolerable financial burden.

I suggested, as the thought went through my mind, that we might consider giving him a 2-meal contract so that he could get his 3rd meal wherever he wanted and get as much protein as he wanted or could find. He wasn't sure that he liked this idea. I told him it was not a definite proposition in any case because it was one that would have to be checked out with various people.

John frankly confessed he wasn't sure how long he would adhere to his vegetarian principles: he thought for a long time and perhaps for a lifetime, but maybe not more than a month or so.

P.S. I forgot John also suggested he be permitted to go into the kitchen and cook his own meals. (He's very good at grilled cheese sandwiches and loves them.) I said I'm sure that couldn't be permitted.

March 11, 1971

FROM: Albert I. Dickerson
TO: Files
SECOND INSTALLMENT: The Vegetarianism of John Smith '74

On March 9, not much to the surprise or delight of the undersigned, the above-named subject sat gloomily down in the chair in my office for further discourse on the above-described topic.

He was a very unhappy young man. He had obviously suffered as much as one could bear, almost, on the diet of the Dartmouth Dining Association.

Mr. Smith was not only sad, he was aggrieved. I'm not too clear —and I don't think he is—about just whom or what he is aggrieved against. But he clearly has grievances against all the people to whom he has talked about his diet problem, and that, to start with, is not a small congregation.

On his first visit he opened up with a quotation from Dean Carroll W. Brewster. It went something like this: "Well, John, you really have been given the runaround, haven't you?" I can just hear Carroll saying that. "Then he talked to me about the grades and then he said, 'Oh, you're a freshman. You should be talking to Dean Dickerson,' and then he sent me across here."

This compassionate response from that man across the hall, the last-man-in-line before the undersigned in this legendary runaround, was a frequent refrain in the present recorded conference.

I was somewhat puzzled by this sense of grievance against all these good people who had listened to his problems. As I look over

12. *The Dean of Freshmen at Moosilauke Ravine Lodge in September 1964.*

this roster, I get a picture of a group of warmhearted, compassionate people who gave him a courteous and sympathetic hearing, before sending him on to the next station. With one exception: Dr. Jackson. This gentleman was not only not warm and sympathetic, but was candidly mad as hell and so indicated in no ambiguous terms when he picked up the telephone in the earshot of Mr. Smith to communicate his utter nausea with all this nonsense to the next man in line, Dean Brewster.

I want all you guys to know that Mr. Smith is impartially mad at you all, with the exception of the good, candid, crustaceous doctor.

How would you feel if you had to survive on "a lettuce sandwich" for lunch every day?

John has managed to work himself up from #24 on the squash ladder to #11 (which barely puts him on the "team" but doesn't get him a numeral). He might have made it close to the top if he had been adequately nourished. In Installment #1, lunches were definitely better than dinners, which were impossible for vegetarians. In the present installment, the situation is reversed.

John's present request is for a contract for breakfasts only. He has been getting up for breakfasts regularly, has been enjoying them, and had completely forgotten his complaint in Installment #1 that the eggs always ran out before the end of the established breakfast period.

"Why should I pay $450 a term for breakfasts, a lettuce sandwich at lunch, and whatever little I can eat at dinner?" he asked.

I am not very good at arithmetic, so I asked John somewhat hesitantly: "Are you really paying $1350 a year for your board at Thayer Hall?"

This question seemed to surprise him. He had made his calculation, apparently, on the per meal prices for non-contract holders.

This gave me what seemed to be the perfect opening for the standard lecture on the Theory and Practice of Contract Dining: namely, it saves you money.

May I here interject a remark to all you deans and ombudsmen who may be reading this memorandum: I think all of us who have to disseminate the facts to students about contract dining and hold the line on regulations should get a regular injection of Truth, at least once a year, from the Business Manager about the real facts of contract dining and the central fact that it won't work unless the rules are observed. Old Pine stump that I am, I have had more instruction in this theology than the younger deans. I believe it, and I can usually convey it with faith and confidence. However, the occasional encounter with a character like Smith sometimes leaves me feeling in the need of a new injection of Faith.

I gave it all to John Smith again. He nodded his head in obvious agreement with every syllable of wisdom I was offering.

But time after time we wound up in exactly the same spot where we started: namely, "There are about 800 other freshmen; and then, there's me."

I told Mr. Smith that I had personally discussed his problem with Mr. Richard W. Olmsted, the Business Manager of the College. (This is the thin line which distinguishes me from all the rest of you heels in the runaround.) I told him that Mr. Olmsted was extremely reluctant to set up special arrangements. I told him that Mr. Olmsted was, however, prepared to give consideration, in his case, on a full-term contract basis only, to a 2-meal-a-day contract, excluding dinner; but with the understanding that the rebate for the dinner would be on the basis of food cost only: i.e., approximately $1.00 per day.

Mr. Smith showed a flicker of interest in this possibility, but it was a very brief flicker. He was back, within a few seconds, with the question: "If you can cut out one meal, why not two?"

What would *you* say in response to such unanswerable logic?

What I said was, roughly, that a 2-meal-a-day contract was at least two-thirds of a contract; breakfast only was no contract at all.

Mr. Smith was not immediately persuaded by this argument. He was not even eventually persuaded by this argument after we had been over it six or nine times.

My buzzer kept buzzing as waiting students piled up for appointments; and my normally dulcet and saintly tone perhaps began to take on a bit of an edge. Anyway, I conveyed the impression that this was the best deal he could expect.

At one point he brightened up a bit as he indulged himself in the fantasy of appearing in Dean Brewster's office early next term, tossing his meal book and board bill in Dean Brewster's face, and exiting triumphantly. I reminded him that if he was constructing a script of this sort, he would have to write me into it in place of Dean Brewster.

During the discussion I repeated my sincere convictions about the resourcefulness and flexibility of the Dartmouth Dining Association in trying to meet the desires and tastes of students. He responded with a warm personal tribute to the "greencoats at Thayer Hall." Nobody, he said with obvious sincerity, could have possibly been more accommodating and nice than the Thayer Hall people who invariably responded to his requests for cereals and other things.

I told John that I had heard that the Thayer Hall administrators, conscious as they were of the fact that John and a few others were seeking to pursue vegetarian diets, had given some thought to the possibility of setting up a vegetarian line in the Dining Hall. I told him that there were obvious difficulties in this, but that I would check to see if there were any new developments on that line.

I think it will be obvious to all readers why I refrained from saying: "John, why don't you go see Mr. Moore?" [Aside to Paul Moore: I hope you will do something nice for me sometime.]

I did not quite push Mr. Smith '74 out of the office, but he left, at least as gloomily as he entered.

He walked darkly out of the office, tresses flowing in the breezes, muttering: "Runaround, runaround, runaround."

I am sending a copy of this to Bill Carter. If the Ombudsman has not yet encountered this problem, he will . . .

If there are any new developments in Thayer Hall which would give solace to Mr. Smith, please advise me. It seems a little odd to me that the vegetarians have not yet united, but they will. Meanwhile, it is perhaps fortunate that in John Smith's world, the Dartmouth Dining Association faces only two problems: (1) John Smith and (2) 2000 other fellows.

A Class of 1972 Romance

January 6, 1969

Dear Sir:

I have been told by Bob, Dartmouth Peagreener, Potter '72 to write you. I am sure you don't remember him, so let me refresh your memory. His many alias' are "The Man," "Gear," "Clyde Barrow," 287569–72, "Babycakes," and sometimes "Dum-Dum."

Bob is a typical "Dartmouth Animal," but I love him. He drinks a little, sleeps a little, studies a lot, smooches a little, and of course eats a lot. He is one of those good-looking, pre-med students with at attaché case full of *Playboys* and a pair of shoes.

Bob loves four things. One—me. Two—His Austin-Healey. Three—running cross-country. And four—Scotch. Sometimes I think he loves his Austin-Healey more than me, and when I tease him about it he gets mad. He thinks that I am going to "do it in"; I just may. Bob doesn't drink much, just Scotch when he can get some.

I am sure that you have heard his big snow job about being president of his senior class, editor of the school paper, and winning various awards. But he does try hard and he puts a lot of time and effort into his studies.

By now you know who I am talking about. I have only one thing to ask. Please take good care of him, because I would like him back in one piece. Thank you.

Sincerely,
Sally Gilman

Note: The names used in the exchange of correspondence are fictitious.—*Editor.*

January 10, 1969

Dear Sally:

President Dickey (alias Sloan John) has been kind enough to share with me your delightful letter about your friend, alias Babycakes '72, or, if you prefer, 287569–72.

Of course I have no way of knowing, Sally, whether you are real or not. Or whether, for that matter, Babycakes is real, either. There is someone who is known to our data processing machinery as 287569–72 and who lives at 200 French Hall, in one of our outlying suburbs. Whether or not this character is one and the same as your Babycakes—or Dum-Dum——or whether he has an Austin-Healey, or whether he most loves it or you or Scotch, is of course unknown to me.

I am sending a copy of this letter to 287569–72. If he is indeed your Babycakes, and is so inclined, I'd be delighted to have him come in for a visit.

If he does, I'll try to explore the priority of his affections. If you are real, and if you're as cute as your letter, you deserve to have him "sent back to you in one piece."

Meanwhile, we can only speculate on the order of his affections. If he's a law-abiding Peagreener, he has to leave that Austin-Healey at home along with you. When he says goodbye to you, how does his behavior compare to when he says goodbye to the Austin-Healey? Whom does he write oftenest?

When you go to the beach, does he run like a hare over hill and dale? Or jog? Or what?

Then there's Carnival. A fellow with Dum-Dum's tastes and habits could obviously afford to ask you to Carnival. Has he? If he hasn't, I'd say you'd better forget the whole thing. He clearly isn't Sincere. In this case I'd refer you to Ann Landers because your problems are obviously beyond the scope of President Dickey, or even me.

And don't let The Man give you any gas about not being able to find you a room for Carnival. My wife and I will give you a room and throw in breakfast.

I suppose it's quite possible that Dum-Dum has similar concerns about you and your college. Has he written to the Chancellor to ask him to check on the situation?

I shall be awaiting the next developments with considerable curiosity.

Sincerely,
Albert I. Dickerson

January 14, 1969

Dear Mr. Dickerson,

In regard to the letter that I received on January 13, 1969, yes, I am very real. My babycakes, who is better known as Bob, is just as real as I am. I hope that he has come to see you. I think he will like you, because I know that I do. I have placed your letter on the closet door just above the two love poems Bob sent to me.

About that Austin-Healey—it stayed at home. If I can't go, neither can it. I didn't know that you could write to an Austin-Healey, but if it can be done, Bob can do it. (At least that is what he says.) I go over and comfort it; it gets lonely too. Bob won't let me drive it; I don't think that he trusts me with his precious car.

About Carnival—I have been asked. Yes, by Dum-Dum. But there is only one small problem—my parents. They think that $150 is too much for Bob to spend on me for a Christmas present. I have decided to talk to them and see if they will let me go if Bob and I split the bill. What I will use for money is another small problem. Not all Texans are rich and own oil wells.

When I think of Hanover and Dallas in the same breath, I always think of money. Heavens, those phone bills will knock you over every time. But it is so easy to say, "Operator, I would like to make a long-distance call." I think it is distantly related to potato chips, once you start, you can't stop. Anyway, the money is seen a lot less around here this semester. (I have a hard time remembering that Washington is on the one dollar bill: I haven't seen one in weeks and weeks.)

I am sure that I will get up to see Dartmouth, and when I do, I would love to stay with you and your wife. As for breakfast, I am very good at washing dishes. Not only that, but I can cook too. I am only a little conceited, but then isn't everybody?

Thank you very much for your letter, and I hope to get another one soon. It is nice to know that you are "looking out" for my Babycakes.

Sincerely,
KOOKY SALLY

January 17, 1969

Dear Kooky Sally:

I was delighted to get your letter of January 14 and to be assured that you are real and that your Babycakes is, too. I've really been looking forward all week to hearing from one or both of you, but I haven't yet heard from Bob. I addressed my letter to #287569 and maybe he didn't get it. I'll try addressing this copy to The Man himself and see if I have better luck, because I would really like to meet him. There are lots of nice things written about him in his admissions folder. My impression is that your judgment isn't bad.

That's a standing invitation to our house which my wife will be delighted to validate at any time with a proper letter of invitation. We have some machinery for washing dishes—antiquated but still operative—but we would like to try your cookery. It surely would be nice if something did work out about Carnival.

If he decides to give me a chance, I will be only too glad to "look out" for your friend.

Yours,
ALBERT I. DICKERSON

January 24, 1969

Dear Sally:

This is just a quick note to tell you that I had a visit with Bob this afternoon, which I enjoyed very much. He's okay and needs no looking out for. I do hope that he will follow through on his promise to drop by for visits periodically.

Yes, we had a chance to talk a little about the Austin-Healey, too, and about the fantastic decorative job you did on it and also about its embarrassing collapse at your dormitory. I was impressed to discover that you were a rally champion.

I'm sorry to hear that there aren't any prospects of seeing you this Carnival, but we'll look forward to a later opportunity.

Sincerely,
ALBERT I. DICKERSON

April 21, 1971

Dear Dean Dickerson:

Remember the spring of 1969 and the crazy young girl who wrote you letters of her "Babycakes" #2875 something? Remember the freshman who took longer to say goodbye to his car than to his girl?

Well, the car has been replaced, but the girl (yes, me!) has a "rock" on her left hand to prove that she will never, ever be replaced.

Yes, sir! The wedding date has been set for August 7 and we Texans are doing it up in style! Ya'll come.

Uncle Sam and the United States Marine Corps have agreed to turn loose of the boy for three weeks. Everyone's invited. (They were beginning to wonder if I would ever catch him—especially when he took up track.)

If you have never been to "Big D," now is your chance. We have plenty of room for guests, etc.!

But Mr. Dickerson, sir, I do have a favor to ask. The original French Hall gang of '68–69 has split up, and I am trying to track a few of them down. Perhaps you could send me their home addresses? I am looking for the following: [five names listed]

I'm not sure you can help, but I adored all these "Dartmouth animals" when I met them and I'd like to find out where they are now. Thank you.

Sincerely,
HONEYWAFFLE
(alias Sally Gilman)

July 7, 1971

Dear Kooky Sally:

When I got back from Europe a short time ago I was delighted to see your letter of April 21 and to learn that Dum-Dum has come through with a rock, and that a date certain has been established on August 7 and that the United States Marine Corps is cooperating.

Yes, I have been to "Big D" and have been impressed by its magnificence; but it won't be possible for me to be there for the nuptials of Honeywaffle Gilman and her Babycakes. But I'll be thinking of you on that date and wishing you a fine wedding and much future happiness.

Where is Bob stationed and what is the nature of his duty? A Navy investigator came through last September to ask about Bob and this makes me wonder whether he was about to be assigned to some sensitive and possibly interesting duty. Give him my very best in your next letter.

I don't know whether you realize it or not, but Bob is a very bright guy and of course his academic performance at Dartmouth never came close to his capacity. This is undoubtedly the reason that he decided to take off some time from college and if the experience of a lot of other people is worth anything, this could prove to have been a very wise decision on Bob's part. When he gets through with his Marine duty, you must make sure that he returns to college, even if you have to support him in the process. I seem to recollect that you were in training for a nursing career and those jobs pay well.

I'll be thinking of you on the Big 7th. Meanwhile, all the best while you wait out the next 31 days.

Sincerely,
ALBERT I. DICKERSON

6. The Parents Letters

Soon after he assumed the position of Dean of Freshmen, Mr. Dickerson began the practice of sending a series of letters to the parents of freshmen throughout the academic year. With some modification, they covered the same basic ground from year to year and in due course became a celebrated part of the Dartmouth literature. The letters printed here are for the year 1971–72.

Parents Letter #1

April 20, 1971

We are happy that your son is one of those selected for admission to Dartmouth with the Class of 1975. I look forward to becoming acquainted with him during the coming year.

I hope that you will look through the booklet on the Freshman Year which has been sent to him, since it has information which will be of interest also to you. If you would like a copy, I should be glad to send one and also to answer any questions that you may have about his plans for his first year.

You will find described in the booklet the various counseling services available to Dartmouth undergraduates. By the time a student begins the Freshman Year, we have gathered a good deal of information about him: from the credentials submitted to the Office of Admissions by the candidate himself, by officials of his school, and by others who write on his behalf; from the forms he will send to this office in the weeks ahead; and from tests administered and interviews held during Freshman Week. The detailed medical histories which incoming students and their family physicians send to our Health Service during the summer are for the confidential use of the Health Service. If there is any health information concerning your son which you think it might be useful for us to have, we would welcome this.

If there is further information that you feel we should have, I should appreciate your writing; indeed, we should be grateful for your writing as fully as you care to, providing insights into the personality and the hopes and aspirations of this young man from those who know him best. Anything you care to write will be read with the utmost care and preserved in confidence, available only to members of this office, faculty advisers, and the College Health Service.

I hope your son will find his Dartmouth experience deeply rewarding, and that you also, in sharing this experience with him during the next four years, will enjoy your associations in the Dartmouth family.

ALBERT I. DICKERSON

Parents Letter #2

August 18, 1971

TO THE PARENTS OF MEMBERS
OF THE CLASS OF 1975

I have been happy to receive letters from many of you in response to my Parents Letter in April. (This was the four-page printed letter expressing pleasure over your son's admission and inviting you to write to me about him.) The present letter is the second in a series of six or seven which I shall send to you during the year, supplementing your letters from your son, in an effort to help you interpret and understand his freshman year experience—a unique and exciting adventure for most. To you who haven't written, I repeat the request that you send along such facts and insights as may help us do a wiser job in counseling your son.

I am enclosing a pamphlet outlining Dartmouth's academic requirements and conduct regulations. This is included in the *Student Handbook* which will be distributed to your sons at the beginning of Freshman Week and will be a subject of discussion during Freshman Week between members of the Interdormitory Council and freshmen. I urge that you and your son read and discuss the material in this document, as well as the material in the booklet *Sources: Their Use and Acknowledgement*.

As I indicated in the pamphlet sent to your son, *Freshman Year 1971–72* (and let me repeat the offer of a copy of that pamphlet for your own use, if you wish it), Dartmouth operates on the assumption that these young men have reached the point where they must begin to make their own decisions and to learn from their own mistakes. It goes without saying that this freedom to make their own choices, which in varying degrees is new to most freshmen, involves both important opportunities and some dangers.

Most freshmen are going through that stage in the approach toward maturity in which they establish the independence of their own personalities. For some, this stage brings emotional stresses. It may also cause some stresses for you, as parents, and may demand considerable understanding on your own part. This important, desirable, and (sooner or later) inevitable stage in the progress to emotional maturity produces temporarily in some young men an assertiveness of ideas which they have adopted as their own, and especially of ideas different from their parents'. To some parents, this phase is disturbing, seeming to nullify eighteen or so years of careful upbringing. Such a negation, most authorities seem to agree, is almost never really what happens in any lasting fashion. In any event, may I ask for your sympathetic understanding if in the next few months or the next four years your son has some hard times, or gives you some hard times, or—as is most frequent in these circumstances—both. (They not infrequently give some hard times to us at the College in the process!)

During the last several years, the media—books, magazines, newspapers, television and radio—have been full of discussion of a generation gap. Perhaps you are beginning to find it all a bit tiresome, as I am. Certainly this is no unique problem of our time. There have been generation gaps since the beginning of civilization. The Old Testament is full of examples, some of them pretty gruesome.

Most modern commentators tend to approach the problem as either (a) a problem of "communication" (another word that has become a rather tiresome cliché) or (b) a conflict of value systems, or both.

As far as communication is concerned, there has surely never been as uninhibited a period in the history of man. You've surely found your sons and daughters all too ready to discuss any topic under the sun. All the old taboos that once inhibited inter-generation conversation have gone out the window. Like most of us, I like to think of myself as shockproof. However, almost a decade ago, I found myself trying to mediate a conflict between a Dartmouth freshman and his mother. I must admit that some of the language she used, in describing the dialogue between her and her son about his relationships with his girl friend, rather startled me. I submit that if there is a communication problem today between the generations, it's a matter of learning to understand and be tolerant of each other's language.

Values are another matter. Many of the analysts and commentators have pointed the finger of blame right at you. They say you are a permissive generation of parents. They say you have no clearly defined value systems of your own that you have imposed on your sons and daughters for them to accept or rebel against. Therefore, they say, your children have flailed around in their various peer groups constructing value systems of their own which, to their delight, have proved so outrageous to you as to fulfill their wildest hopes and expectations.

I don't accept this as a generalization with respect to parents of Dartmouth freshmen. I have observed situations where it seems to be true. But just as when I started deaning freshmen a dozen or so years ago, I find entering freshmen in general a group of engaging young men with good principles; and when I see them graduating four years later, a good deal more mature and sophisticated than when they entered—as they should be—they are still engaging young men; and their principles, somewhat modified with respect to life goals as many are, equally respectworthy and often more so.

Remembering Hamlet's observation that "there is nothing either good or bad but thinking makes it so," I suggest that if we start out with the assumption that there is a generation gap, there will be one. On the other hand, I believe that if you and your sons and we teachers and administrators at Dartmouth start out with the belief that we can understand each other if we try, we will.

The best parts of this series of letters to parents in past years have been the comments and reflections which parents have sent to me and which I have shared with others through these letters. I shall be grateful for your comments as we proceed through the year.

Probably many of you saw the memorandum sent to your sons by Mr. Chamberlain, Director of Admissions, on April 17, accompanying their certificates of admission. Attached to this memorandum were reprints of official texts describing the Honor Principle and the policy on Freedom of Expression and Dissent. Mr. Chamberlain's memorandum to your sons said: "Please read carefully on the following pages two primary principles under which Dartmouth operates. Your subscription to them will be assumed by your statement of intention to enroll." To get these two important principles before you for joint consideration with your sons, may I reprint them here:

THE HONOR PRINCIPLE

Fundamental to the principle of independent learning is the requirement of honesty and integrity in the performance of academic assignments, both in the classroom and outside. Accordingly, Dartmouth operates on the principle of academic honor, without proctoring of tests and examinations. A man who submits work which is not his own forfeits his opportunity to continue at Dartmouth.

The Honor Principle depends on the willingness of students, individually and collectively, to maintain and perpetuate standards of academic honesty. Each student accepts the responsibility not only to be honorable in his own academic affairs but also to support the principle as it applies to others.

A student who becomes aware of a violation of this Principle is bound by honor to take some action. He may report the violation, speak personally to the student, exercise some form of social sanction, or do whatever is appropriate under the circumstances. If he stands by and does nothing, he threatens both the spirit and the operation of the principle of academic honor.

Examinations No student shall give or receive assistance in an examination or written quiz.

Papers Any form of plagiarism is dishonest. College standards have been set forth in detail in the pamphlet *Sources: Their Use and Acknowledgement.*

Library Use No student may infringe upon the right of others to have fair and equal access to library resources. Failure to sign for material taken from the library and similar abuse of library privileges is considered academic dishonesty.

POLICY REGARDING FREEDOM OF EXPRESSION AND DISSENT

The following principle has been adopted by vote of the faculty, Board of Trustees and appropriate agencies of the undergraduate body:

> Dartmouth College prizes and defends the right of free speech, and the freedom of the individual to make his own decisions, while at the same time recognizing that such freedom exists in the context of law and of responsibility for one's actions. The exercise of these rights must not deny the same rights to any other individual. The College therefore both fosters and protects the rights of individuals to express dissent. Protest or demonstration shall not be discouraged, so long as neither force nor the threat of force is used, and so long as the orderly processes of the College are not deliberately obstructed.

In voting adoption of this policy statement, the Faculty also voted the following implementing action:

> That the Faculty of Arts and Sciences requests the Officers of the College, and all appropriate agencies of the Faculty and the student body, to communicate this policy to all segments of the Dartmouth community in such a way that it may be understood that membership in this community carries with it, as a necessary condition, the agreement to honor and abide by this policy.

With respect to the Honor Principle and academic propriety, a number of students in the recent past, who have found themselves in disciplinary difficulties for academic dishonesty, have sought to justify their actions with the claim that they did not realize that failure to acknowledge indebtedness was plagiarism. Their high schools assigned so-called "research themes" that were in fact a potpourri of unacknowledged ideas and quotations. Dartmouth's expectations in this regard are set forth in *Sources: Their Use and Acknowledgement*. These are of the utmost importance. The *Sources* pamphlet has markedly reduced the number of penalties for plagiarism. I encourage you to urge your son to seek the counsel of his teachers at Dartmouth if he is in any doubt whatever about the proprieties of scholarship. In the discharge of all his academic responsibilities, he will be working within the climate of Dartmouth's honor principle.

The desire to excel is a worthy one, but a new perspective is required when several hundred young men who are accustomed to excelling among their school groups come together on a college campus in a kind of competition which they have not faced before. The problem of *survival* is not as acute as many freshmen fear: we normally lose by academic failure only one or two men out of about 800 in the first two terms; and almost invariably this is the result of immature use of freedom rather than any inadequacy of ability or preparation. But excelling is, by definition, for the few; and the A's and B's to which our students have become accustomed in secondary school are sparingly granted by college instructors.

Many a young man has been saved from the tragedy of taking disastrous shortcuts by knowing, in the deep direct way which comes only through intimate conversation, that his parents do not expect him to excel—or even stay in college—at such a cost to himself.

The question of drug abuse is one which is certainly not new to you, as it has recently become a serious problem in high schools and preparatory schools as well as in the universities. The enclosed College pamphlet includes the regulation on Drugs (page 16) and a summary of laws governing drug use in New Hampshire (page 25).

These items deserve the closest attention of your sons and yourselves.

With regard to automobiles, you undoubtedly are already aware that freshmen are not permitted to own, maintain or operate motor vehicles in Hanover or its vicinity. We shall appreciate your cooperation in the observance of this regulation. The regulation purposely avoids a precise definition of "vicinity." For example, a student from western New York once inquired whether garaging his car in Woodstock (18 miles) would be in violation, or whether he should choose Rutland (45 miles). Maintaining a car in either place would have been in violation. On the other hand, a freshman who relieved a sleepy upperclassman at the wheel and drove right to the door of Topliff Hall if apprehended would probably be commended for his good judgment rather than disciplined for his violation. Last year the Committee on the Freshman Class voted, on an experimental basis for one year only, to permit freshmen in good academic standing to bring cars to campus during the spring term. Only 58 did so. This experiment has not yet been evaluated. Meanwhile, local parking problems continue to grow more acute. Whether this permission will be granted to the Class of 1975 will remain a matter of doubt until the Committee reviews the question during the winter.

The regulations governing the use of intoxicating beverages reflect the careful thinking of many here—including teachers, administrators, parents, and undergraduate leaders—concerning a problem that is older than the oldest university and indeed as old as civilization. Prohibition of student drinking has been tried on many campuses, including this one, with the widely accepted conclusion that, while campus prohibition may tend to conceal drinking somewhat, it is more likely to exaggerate the problem than to cure it, with the further observation that unenforceable regulation is very poor education. Our regulations represent our intention to hold those Dartmouth students who do drink (many do not) to standards of responsible, mature conduct with regard to drinking as well as other things. It is important that you and your son understand that intoxication is regarded and treated as grave misconduct at Dartmouth.

I believe that your careful consideration of the College's standards and regulations, jointly with your son, can be helpful to him, to us, and to you. We must recognize that the ability of a college to exercise a controlling influence on the habits and deportment of individual students is limited, however determined it may be that all its institutional influences should be good ones. Behavior patterns are pretty largely formed by age 18. This is particularly true with respect to the young man's consideration for other people wherein the habits previously formed, with occasional exceptions, continue dominant.

At a somewhat superficial level of consideration for others, I might mention the simple amenities of letter-writing. Faculty advisers have reported to me with understandable shock that some freshmen whom they have invited to dinner have failed even to acknowledge the invitation; and larger numbers neglect to give appropriate expression of their appreciation afterward. A parting reiteration from parents to sons of what has been inculcated in the home in these matters might be in order.

If I thought it would do any good, I would urge you to urge your sons to organize their lives at college in order to get adequate sleep. However, I have about concluded that nothing that you may tell them or that I may tell them will have any immediate effect. For most freshmen, this is the first time in their lives when nobody pays any attention to the time they go to bed. Many of them, therefore, spend their first college months trying to outdo one another in "late booking." Many of them appear in my office for conferences looking sleepy, pale, and bleary-eyed, ready to boast about how little sleep they get, about the number of "all-nighters" they've put in during the past week. Sooner or later, they discover that this does not really pay off in grades or in any other way; but experience seems to be the only way they discover this. Surveys conducted by the student radio station continue to show that freshmen stay up later than upperclassmen.

Certainly, learning the mature uses of freedom is the greatest challenge of the first college year. The most valuable wisdom your son will gain during the coming months will be learned in the process of

13. With administrative colleagues at Moosilauke Ravine Lodge in 1968. Left to right, Secretary of the College Sidney C. Hayward, Dean of the College Thaddeus Seymour, Dean Dickerson, Dean of Summer Programs Waldo Chamberlin, and President John Sloan Dickey. Below: Dean Dickerson in 1970 with students participating in the Bridge Program.

making the many kinds of *choices* that he will have to make from day to day.

Undoubtedly you have been watching the newspapers, as we have, concerning the slow progress of new Selective Service legislation. As you may know, the House passed the Senate-House Conference version of the Bill in early August, but the Senate did not act upon it before the month-long adjournment. Apparently the Bill, if passed, will end all student deferment, and those drafted while attending college would only be permitted to complete the term or semester in which they are currently enrolled. However, this is simply speculation until some legislation is enacted. Your sons will be given the most recent available information about the draft during Freshman Week draft counseling sessions. The College's Counselor on Student Military Problems, Professor James F. Cusick, is available for advice and information throughout the year at the Office of Student Services.

At the opening of Freshman Week, the College will open a "Parents Lounge" in the Top of the Hop in Hopkins Center for the convenience of visiting parents at the following times:

    Wednesday, September 15   Noon to 7:00 p.m.
    Thursday, September 16   9:30 a.m.–3:30 p.m.

To you fathers, may I suggest that you circle February 18–20 on your calendars as Freshman Fathers Weekend. This is an occasion arranged and conducted by the officers of the freshman class, and in due course their invitation will be sent to you.

Let me now introduce my colleagues with whom you may have contacts as you visit, write or telephone during the year. The Associate Dean of Freshmen is Ralph N. Manuel, a Dartmouth alumnus who, after his graduation in 1958, served a tour of duty as an officer in the United States Navy. At the conclusion of his Navy service he was invited back to Dartmouth as Assistant Director of Admissions. He has just returned to Dartmouth after three years at the University of Illinois where he was engaged in graduate study and in student counseling. He is a native of Frederick, Maryland. Mrs.

Katharine Brock is Assistant to the Dean of Freshmen. In addition to independent administrative responsibilities, she also serves as my private secretary. Mrs. Aldis Dow is Registrar of Freshmen. Mrs. Vita Mark is secretary to Dean Manuel and has other independent responsibilities. All of these ladies share with you the experience and responsibilities of being parents.

I am afraid that this has been a pretty solemn letter, for the most part. This is hardly appropriate, because there is a great deal that is fun in the freshman year, and not a little that is funny, both for the freshmen and for people like you and me who will be sharing their experiences vicariously. You will find some lighter notes in later letters, most of which have been contributed by parents who have responded with humor to the challenges of being fathers or mothers of freshmen. A couple of years back, we had one such from a parent even before the son's arrival:

> Rarely is a parent asked to write about his own child so I cannot allow this opportunity to pass without a reply to your kind invitation. I don't want to tell you too much about Hank because I would rather he come as a complete surprise.
>
> From your letter, I gather you already know more about Hank than we do. Of course you cannot know that he can put up a tent in record time and follow that feat by pumping up two air mattresses simultaneously—one with a hand pump and the other with a foot pump. He tried doing three at one time (blowing into the third by mouth) but that proved too slow. He can crack open a coconut with proficiency, and he has an uncanny sense which enables him to disappear whenever there is any work to be done around the house.
>
> Naturally we love him very much. Are you sure you're ready?

We were ready for Hank and his classmates, and we're looking forward to your son and his.

Sincerely yours,
ALBERT I. DICKERSON

P.S. Since you and your sons are presumably reading this letter together, I perhaps should make it clear both to them and to you that I regard *them* as my primary "clients." If they entrust confidences to me, I must be scrupulous in respecting such confidences. I strive toward keeping everything candid and aboveboard between them and you and me, and I try never to say anything to a parent that I would not say or have not said to the son.

Parents Letter #3

November 15, 1971

Dear Parents of '75:

This letter is primarily to accompany mid-term reports in courses in which your sons are standing at "unsatisfactory" levels—i.e., "D" or "E." If the normal experience of the past several years prevails, a half to a third of you will find one or more such reports in this letter. To those of you who receive reports, I want to give a little background for realistic appraisal of your sons' situations.

Even among those of you whose sons have not received any of these mid-term reports, I know that in recent weeks many have received worried or frustrated letters from their sons. The majority of freshmen have been finding, during the recent wave of hour examinations, that more academic effort than they have ever previously exerted is producing grades in the C range. This is normal.

To all of you I should like to give a brief report on the first two months of your sons' freshman year at Dartmouth.

MID-TERM GRADES

At mid-term, in order that students may check their scholastic standing in their respective courses in time to improve their work if it is at an unsatisfactory level, instructors report advisory grades of freshmen standing D or E. (No higher grades are reported at this time.) Normally, as is indicated above, barely more than half of the members of the Freshman Class pass mid-terms without any E's or D's. In the last three classes, which had exceptionally good records, better than two-thirds of the freshmen escaped mid-term reports at this time. If you do not find a card enclosed with this letter (and I can see you shaking the envelope now) it means that your son is one of these and is currently standing C— or better in all of his courses (unless we have inserted a slip in a wrong envelope, which, alas, we almost always do among the Joneses and Smiths). This is the way they look:

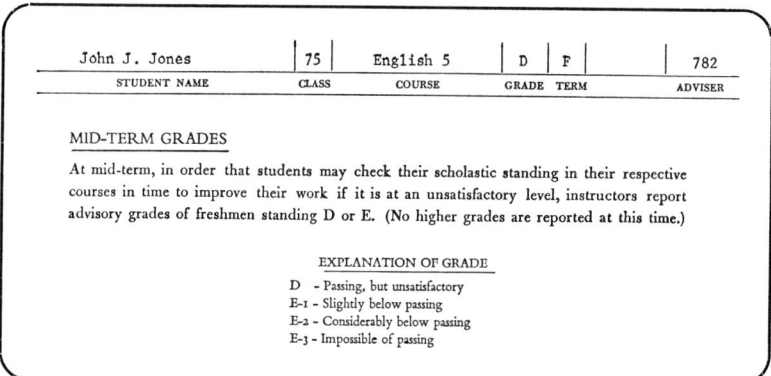

The cards which are enclosed show grades lower than C—. The grade of D is considered unsatisfactory but passing. E-1 is slightly below passing and E-2 considerably below passing. It is assumed to be next to hopeless for a man to achieve a passing grade in a course in which he stands E-3 at mid-term. A man receiving a grade of E-3 should promptly discuss with his instructor and with me or Dean Manuel the desirability of dropping the course and taking a failing grade in it, in order to concentrate on his other courses.

With honest effort, most low mid-term grades can be pulled up to a satisfactory level, and the majority of them are. For example, you may be interested in these figures concerning last fall's mid-term grades compared to final grades for the fall term. Of all the mid-term D's, 67.4% were converted to final grades of C— or better; 26.3% remained at D; 6.3% dropped to final E's.

Among mid-term E-1's, 37.5% were converted to final grades of C— or better; 66.6% were converted to a final grade of D or better;

and 33.3% remained at the failing level. Among mid-term E-2's, 28.6% finally passed.

These figures are quoted to show what application and self-discipline can and do accomplish after mid-term for students of low standing at that time, with the help of their growing skill in handling college courses and in using time efficiently. The latter is the most important lesson learned during the beginning terms at college.

For those who have a particular need of developing these skills, the Office of Student Counseling offers assistance throughout the year, in individual counseling about students' particular problems in relation to their reading and study skills and in laboratory sessions designed to improve reading and study techniques. I have invited those freshmen who have two or three mid-term reports to sign up for this program.

ADVANCE CREDITS AND EXEMPTIONS

Another type of enclosure which some of you will find in this envelope (shake it again!) is a different form of IBM card which shows credits and/or exemptions which have been granted to your son on admission. To avoid repetition of work already well done in secondary school, Dartmouth for a good many years has recognized exceptional preparation among its incoming freshmen.

Course *credit* for one or more term courses is given to those freshmen who at or before entrance present satisfactory evidence of college-level competence in any subject in the Dartmouth curriculum. Such credit does not carry any grade (or "quality points") with it, but does count as a course (unit) passed.

Many entering freshmen have studied a subject thoroughly enough in high school to gain a solid introduction to a discipline, even though their level is less than that required for Dartmouth course credit. For such students a proficiency *exemption* is granted. An exemption carries with it a reduction in the distributive requirements by one term course in a particular discipline. (Dartmouth's requirements for the B.A. degree include four courses in humanities, four in the sciences, and four in the social sciences.) This allows a student wider choice by freeing him from one or more of the specific degree requirements and gives him entry into more advanced courses. If you would like more detailed information, please write us for the pamphlet *Recognition of Exceptional Preparation.*

ABOUT WORRYING

As I observed in the opening paragraphs, there are a good many students without any D's or E's who are doing their share of worrying. You may remember that I forecast this prospective experience in my August letter. There is considerable shock for many Dartmouth students, who have been accustomed to receiving only A's and B's in secondary school and perhaps without a great deal of effort, to find in some or possibly in all their Dartmouth courses that they are working extremely hard and receiving mediocre or inferior grades because of lack of experience with college-type examinations, inadequate training in writing, unfamiliarity with new types of subject matter, need for practice in the organization of college-level work, or inexperience with the quantity and quality of work expected by college teachers.

Let me add two or three more observations about this business of worrying. The first is that it is a normal, and probably in general a quite wholesome phenomenon of the freshman year. It is the blithely unworried among the relatively low hangers who worry me. They are most often the ones who come a cropper. The others who are "running scared," as long as they don't panic (and few do), are most often the ones who win out. Of course, when one encounters a badly worried freshman, one cannot help sharing the distress that his parents feel; and I must say that every fall I am re-impressed by the responsiveness of Dartmouth teachers to the needs of such students for encouragement and help. However, I sometimes ask myself this question: suppose a college—through engaging a massive corps of counselors and hand-holders and by utilizing all of the ingenious devices, overt and subliminal, that psychologists could dream up—

should be able, without lowering academic standards, to remove all of the stresses from the college experience: would this be a good thing? I suspect that a lot of the growing which is done during this period might not take place without the stresses that are a normal part of the experience.

THE LETTER HOME

Another general observation about the worrying business is that the typical "letter home" tends, usually quite unintentionally, to picture things as somewhat bleaker than they are. I think this, too, is a wholesome thing: that a student can unburden himself of his anxieties in his letters home and then, somewhat purged of worry for the nonce, go about his business with more or less normal equilibrium. More often than not, when the "letters home" suggest to understandably distressed parents that the student may be on the verge of a crack-up, on the campus scene he is going about his business with normal poise. In conference, his anxieties will usually prove sincere and genuine; but when encountered with his companions on the street or in the dining hall, he will look thoroughly chipper and healthy.

If your son has written or telephoned you suggesting that he should perhaps leave Dartmouth and transfer to another college, you should not regard this as a rare or exceptionally worrisome thing. Letters of this sort are dispatched homewards by freshmen in some numbers every autumn from every college in the land. By this time of year, Dean Manuel and I normally have already heard this question discussed by several freshmen, and one feels sure that others are talking to their friends and writing home about it.

I'm sure I don't need to spell out the reasons. I shall have more to say on this subject in a later letter, in reference to what I call the "January Syndrome." Briefly, every college student comes from a school and community in which he has had recognition. He has been recognized and, more often than not, considerably respected for his particular qualities and talents. He arrives on a college campus with some hundreds of fellow-freshmen, all equally bereft of status. Inevitably, they will wonder how they are going to measure up in this new group, which is larger in most cases than were their school groups and is known to be selective. Unless one is totally lacking in sensitivity and humility, there will be some self-analysis and anxiety. One student, in the first week of college, came right to the point. "Sir," he said, "I don't think I should be here. I've been talking to these guys who got all A's without cracking a book. Now, *I* had to work for my grades, and they weren't all A's, either." I told him I was confident of his success (which I was, and events proved me right) but probably we ought to worry about his friends. Others approach the question of belonging here less directly, talking about their health, some especially good course offered by the college back home, etc.

A word on the subject of "flunking out"—a phrase somewhat loosely used by freshmen during the mid-term period. Only a man with final failures in all three courses would normally even be considered for suspension at the end of the first term. It seems fully possible that there will be none such. Two course failures would result in probation. One failure plus one D will result in an academic warning. The tolerances for adjustment and getting on one's feet are broad during this first term: for example, a man with two C—'s and one failure will be, technically, in "good standing" at the end of the term, although he could not safely continue at that level of achievement.

Some freshmen have a way of referring to mid-term reports as "warnings." These reports are, in a sense, unofficial warnings that the level of work to date in those courses is unsatisfactory. But these reports at mid-term are not *grades*, and do *not* become part of the permanent record, and are *not* to be confused with "official college warnings" for unsatisfactory scholarship.

Although it may be presumptuous of me to suggest what should be your reaction to the mid-term reports of your son herein reported, our experience is that the great majority need sympathy, understanding, and encouragement more than they need chiding and exhortation. If your son is already worried, it does not help to add your anxiety to his.

Exhortation, however, may be in order for your son if his past pattern of academic behavior has reflected sporadic attention to his studies and achievement clearly below his abilities; or if you have reason to believe that he has been doing less than his best at Dartmouth this fall, has taken too many "road trips," or otherwise through lack of sustained effort has failed by his own neglect to live up to your and our expectations of him. It would be appropriate for you to encourage your son to take advantage of the counseling services available to him and to see me or Dean Manuel if he is in any difficulty.

TRANSPORTATION

I hope you will use your influence against your son's planning too tight a travel schedule coming and going for his winter and spring holidays, whether he is traveling by plane, train, bus or automobile. If the latter, he will be dependent on others, but even here influence can be exerted. It is encouraging to note in this college generation an increasing sobriety over the perils of automobile travel: although students cover considerable distances in surprisingly short time, it is standard procedure to keep one passenger awake to talk to the driver, to shift drivers at frequent intervals, to use seat belts, etc., and the adolescent urge to speed for speed's sake has been generally outgrown. But the optimistic inclination of youth tends not to take into account the unpredictability of weather from November to April everywhere, and especially in the north-east. Weather can knock the most reasonable travel schedules, whether by plane or car, into a cocked hat, and it frequently does. For those who are pushing to meet a *tight* schedule, unnecessary hazards are undertaken.

Registration for the next term is from 1:30 to 4:30 and 7:00 to 10:00 in the afternoon and evening of Sunday, January 2.

Looking ahead a bit, experience leads us to expect that between now and June several dozen freshmen will come in with requests, for extraordinarily varied reasons, for permission to brings cars to the campus, even though there are well-known regulations against this. Some freshmen will mistakenly assume that it is permissible for them to bring cars temporarily and have them impounded here. This is not permitted, unless authorized by this office *in advance*. If any number of these requests were granted, the number of petitioners would certainly multiply astonishingly. One of the perennial diversions of this office is to admire the variety and ingenuity of these requests and the good humor of the usual parting remark: "That's what I thought you'd say, but it doesn't hurt to try . . ." One would be callous not to sympathize with the logistical problem of the seasonal home-campus-home transportation of those vast quantities of clothing, sports paraphernalia, electronic equipment, etc., etc.,; but . . . .

A GOOD BEGINNING

Having been concerned earlier in this letter with the anxieties which constitute a normal part of the first weeks of college, in the hope of relieving some of these concerns, let me turn now to some of the things which make us feel that this has been a good fall at Dartmouth.

The letters home have surely commented, invariably and with emphasis, on how hard the writers are working, on how intensively they are "booking." Allowing a little for the hyperbole which is customary in the "Dear Mom and Dad" form of literature, there is a good deal of truth in the accounts you have received. Freshmen find very quickly that their instructors expect a good deal more work of them than did their secondary school teachers. A great many of them are genuinely puzzled for a while in trying to figure out "what the prof wants." Much of the content of some courses is of an unfamiliar kind with which they have not previously had to deal.

When we speak this early in the year of the Class of 1975 appearing to be a good class off to a good start, it is of course an impressionistic comment—reporting the impressions conveyed to us by teachers, faculty advisers, members of the Interdormitory Council, leaders of the Outing Club's Freshman Trip and other upperclassmen.

One of the qualities mentioned with unusual frequency with respect to the new class is its maturity. Perhaps this is an observation that one should not dwell on publicly. I have discovered that some young men bristle at this kind of praise. They seem to figure that it is somehow an insult to be accorded this kind of approval by the Older Generation and that there must be something wrong with them if they earn it. However, this comment with respect to '75 has been offered frequently by their fellow-students of the three upper classes. Several of us have also received the impression that this is a very good-humored class, one which is wearing very few chips on its shoulders. Perhaps this pleasant ambience is partly due to the fact that we have enjoyed an unusually extended and beautiful Indian Summer (which was abruptly terminated by three inches of snow the other day). Everybody also enjoyed the series of cliff-hanging football victories, until Columbia stopped that string. The best freshman soccer team in years has just finished an unbeaten season, the first since 1953. The "A" freshman football team has lost only to Yale, with one game to go . . . However, the Class of 1975 has not really distinguished itself so far in bonfire building, even though a few hardy souls, including upperclassmen and a few deans, erected a whopper for the Yale game . . . The '75 Freshman Council is now being elected and the class will soon be in business.

Just to provide you with a bit of the flavor of life in Hanover in November, I asked Peter Smith, General Administrator of the Hopkins Center, to run off extra copies of "November at the Hopkins Center" for enclosure with this letter.

Soon after Freshman Week a few years ago, a parent called to my attention a poem published in *Harper's Magazine* which I am now sharing with you, on the chance that you may have felt some of these sentiments since depositing your '75 in September:

Computations After Depositing One Freshman

A classic sum of sun and elms
Arched neatly over his new world
But our exchange of blunt farewells
Was little like our large intent,
With habit there as subtrahend.
The ride back was longer by just
One driver less but seemed like more.
And now a younger son becomes
An Elder, postulating all
From his new quarters voice and chores.
The cat expands, the dog declines.
The mother nervously negates
All talk about that other world
Except when she is counting socks.
And now accrues to us more house,
More cars, more television sets,
More meals from a roast, more peace and quiet
Than we really need.

                                E. A. Muir

        Sincerely yours,
        ALBERT I. DICKERSON

Parents Letter #4

December 22, 1971

Dear Parents of '75:

First, let me wish to you, and to your '75 sons who are our bond of mutual interest and concern, a Merry Christmas and a very good New Year. Most of you will still be together when this letter reaches you—unless something unexpected happens between this writing and the scheduled mailing date, or in the vagaries of the mails thereafter.

FIRST TERM GRADE REPORTS

Since this letter is written to accompany the grade reports of your sons (his copy of his grade report is being sent to him at his campus mail address), we should say something about first-term grades. Very likely there is in your home at this moment too intense a concern about *grades*: too intense for a variety of reasons in a variety of situations, but, speaking more generally, because (a) grades are never a precise measure of learning and (b) grades for the first ten weeks of a student's college career are often a very imperfect measure of his intellectual potential or his effort.

Perhaps the enclosed grade reports won't mean much to you without some frame of reference. (I discovered this when I got an IBM grade report like the enclosed for one of my sons who went to another college, without any explanation: this is one of the reasons why these Parents Letters have been concocted.) Based on the experience of recent years, the breakpoint between the quarters of the Class of 1975 on the basis of point average will be: top quarter: 5.0–4.0;

second quarter: 4.0–3.7; third quarter; 3.7–3.0; lowest quarter 3.0 and below.

In a "Happy New Year" letter like this one, it would be nice if all these reports could be straight A's, but there will be only about a dozen or two of these.

If your son has always up to now been in the highest quarter in school (as most of them have) and now appears in one of the lower quarters (as three quarters of them do), I can only remind you that he is working now as a member of a rather carefully selected group of students whose range of ability is much higher and narrower than the range of abilities of students in almost any secondary school; and only one-fourth of them can be in the top quarter! Some of us do our sons little justice by holding up to them unreasonable standards of achievement: sometimes, perhaps, because we achieved at that level ourselves; often because we didn't and are looking to him to realize our unrealized ambitions. The compassion of college counselors and deans is spent in largest measure on the student who is pushing himself as hard as he can and being pressured by parents for higher grades than he is earning.

Many of us who make up American society pay little daily heed in the family circle to the life of the mind and to excellence in its exercise. If your sons and daughters combine qualities of competitiveness and competence, they may "compete" themselves into selective colleges and arrive on the campuses without any real understanding of why they are there. If this happens and they get to college without any real feeling of the importance of intellectual exercise for its own sake, this is not their fault, but ours. Certainly the colleges contain more students whose motivations are either of the wrong kind or are insufficient in degree than society can afford. (The undermotivated ones are affectionately known as "loose hangers" in the undergraduate vernacular.)

THE JANUARY SYNDROME

As you receive this, your son will be thinking about his return to Hanover and may indeed be on his way. This is therefore an appropriate time for description of what I call the January Wish-I-Were-Somewhere-Else Syndrome, to which I alluded in the November letter. This is a phenomenon which will be manifesting itself in residential colleges all over the country during the next few weeks. Happily for Dartmouth, the calendar of our three-term, three-course program removes one of the main elements of the syndrome. Your son came home for the holidays with his first college finals under his belt. They weren't anywhere near as traumatic an experience as the sophomores had made him believe. The fact that these first finals are now behind him, for better or for worse, gives the Dartmouth freshman a welcome feeling of relief and of belonging.

But speaking generally, the campus-bound freshman as January approaches is not a happy man. Home had never looked so good to him. You were never so liberal with the keys to the car. The brothers and sisters, if any, were never so indulgent. As for the girl, either (a) *she* never looked so good, or (b) they broke off, or (c) the worst happened and *both* of these things occurred. (The latter is known as being "shot down.") None of these three eventualities tends to cheer the student in January as he sets off to return to his college campus. The sense of adventure and discovery which dominated the September departure is missing. In its place is a sort of delayed homesickness. So . . . the freshman, having vastly enjoyed the all-too-brief hometown exhilaration of being The Returned College Man, goes back to college to face, under most college calendars, the culmination of all his academic insecurities as the dreaded finals approach. Even the Dartmouth freshman, with that particular ordeal behind him, turns his face toward Hanover with a sobering sense of still having his way to make as a college man.

So in January in residential colleges everywhere, freshman deans are talking to freshmen who come in to say they think they should quit college, or transfer; go to work, or join the army, or travel. They talk about their health, their sinuses, the climate; about your health or business problems, or the illness of aunts or grandparents; they yearn for the life of the big city (whether or not they have ever lived in one); they have suddenly discovered that a college nearer home (where possibly a particular girl happens to be attending or planning to enroll) offers courses especially well adapted to their suddenly discovered needs; etc., etc. Things they never mention are (a) homesickness and (b) worry over finals.

For this description of the January Wish-I-Were-Somewhere-Else Snydrome, I have drawn on various colleagues at other colleges. It's a comfort to all of us to realize how universal this experience is.

HAVE THEY BEEN HAPPY HOLIDAYS?

Our calendar provides a Christmas recess of generous length, but even so you probably will not need all your fingers to count up all your son's evenings at home. Indeed, I surmise you would not find it mathematically too difficult to compute the total of waking hours spent under the family roof, especially if you eliminate those spent at the table and around the refrigerator.

With your sons perhaps at home to read over your shoulders, I hope to sound not too flippant about the foibles of freshmanism. However, one of the many fine qualities of the typical freshman is his honesty and candor, and I am sure he will not mind a few general observations concerning characteristics of his age group that may irritate or amuse his elders. After all, parents are People and they are entitled to a Point of View. The main purpose of these letters, beyond the transmission of grades and other essential information, is to make a modest effort at strengthening the insights and the understanding between home and campus; and in this effort I try never to say to a parent anything I would not be prepared to say to the son, or vice versa.

So let's face it: a college freshman is likely to be a pretty self-centered fellow. At the freshman's age and in this once-in-a-lifetime situation of feeling that one must make his place quickly in a new peer group of substantial size and of high and varied abilities, there is a great deal of self-questioning; of self-evaluation in relation to academic challenges, in relation to fellow-students, in relation to girls, in relation to everything. In simple fact, freshmen spend a lot of time thinking about themselves. It is understandable if parents, in the face of this sometimes massive self-preoccupation, occasionally feel rebuffed. It is an odd but widely recognized fact that it never occurs to young men of this age, who are themselves extremely sensitive to criticism from their families, that parents also have feelings, and can also be sensitive about being "wanted" or being treated with bare toleration.

Some of you have observed, usually with more amusement than irritation, exaggerated assertions of independence by word or deed by these young men who know as well as you do (hence the instinct to assertiveness) their degree of continuing dependence in more than just the financial sense. If some of your freshman sons seem to have all the answers, I can only warn: wait until they are sophomores!

Occasionally tensions build up during the first long vacation and threaten a serious break between the student and his family. "How would *you* feel," I asked a freshman in one of these situations, "if *your* son, after having spent only five evenings at home in a three-week vacation, disappeared entirely from the family ken for his last days—including New Year's Eve—and dashed home from the Rose Bowl with just enough time to pick up his suitcase and add a few final touches to the chaos of his room before rushing off with friends to the airport?"

Well, things usually work out a little better than that and leave a tolerant afterglow of loving amusement behind them. Take as an example this letter which a mother wrote me during a recent January in response to that year's version of this Parents Letter:

> Yes, indeed, the College Man returned! He visited his high school making sure to wear his 'Dartmouth' jacket although the weather called for the winter coat; and from his talk I later gathered that he made quite an impression. He visited his former French teacher, giving her suggestions which she appreciated, of course. My own ego is only beginning to inflate since his departure. My grammar has been corrected; world events have been explained to me with great patience; and in simple language I have been psychoanalyzed daily. How I ever managed to get through college and hold down a fairly responsible

job is still a mystery to me but much more so to him! Yes, it's amazing how much they learn in four short months of college.

However, I noted a change in him. Living with eight boys has made him more considerate. He waits on himself without complaint and is much nicer to live with . . .

SINCE THE LAST LETTER...

As this is being written a few days in advance of its scheduled mailing, grades are being tabulated and analyzed and there's no way of guessing what '75's final record for the term will be, but its mid-term record was good. You'll remember that in the November letter I predicted that almost half of the class would get at least one D or E. As it turned out, only 147 out of 812 received one or more reports. Reported in one subject, 131; in two, 11; in three, 5. Total: 147. The Class of 1974, of comparable size, showed, respectively, 110, 13 and 1 for a total of 124.

The Freshman Council was established in November, with a representative and an alternate representative from each dormitory. The organization meeting was conducted by Dunham Jewett '72, president of the Interdormitory Council. The Freshman Fathers Weekend Committee was designated at this meeting and Calvin Thomas, at a later meeting, was elected chairman of the committee. You fathers presumably have received your invitations to this event, February 18–20, and we all hope you are planning to attend in record numbers.

THANKS TO YOU

I want to thank many of you for your letters, some of which are still on my desk awaiting reply. The "form letter" is probably the least satisfactory medium of human communication, and it is a tribute to your fine understanding that some of you have responded in such warmly friendly and personal ways to these letters.

Dean Manuel joins me in wishing the best in 1972 for *all* of you.

Sincerely yours,
ALBERT I. DICKERSON

Parents Letter #5

February 14, 1972

Dear '75 Parents:

This letter is being written in the quietude which sets in after Winter Carnival. During the ten days preceding this snowy fiesta, Dartmouth breaks out in a rash of hour exams. Then the faculty, with a generosity regarded by undergraduates as less than excessive, grants a 36-hour Carnival holiday, beginning Thursday night. The letter-writing, telegraphing, long-distance-telephoning, room-getting, ticket-buying, general arranging and anticipating which precede Carnival; the intense activity and non-sleeping which are Carnival; and the recuperation and reminiscence which follow it: these all add up to several times 36.

So as this week opens, a chill hush envelops the campus. The activity known as Heavy Booking is being talked about, as something about to be begun . . . In the succession of cycles in campus morale we have, about now, a minor dip which we could call the post-Carnival syndrome, were it not for fear of overdoing this syndrome bit and inventing some which might never occur if we didn't talk about them. These famous winter festivals are always followed by bull sessions in which the prospect of the work-a-day, non-Carnival Dartmouth is viewed with despair. Comparisons are made with other institutions which do not inflict on their students such interminably bleak stretches of monastic industry as exist here between Carnivals. About now a handful of freshmen will find that they are getting debilitated by the grade famine after the rich diet of high school grades they've been accustomed to, and the family phone bills will leap up again. The appearance now of mid-term reports does not brighten the horizon of those students and their correspondents.

MID-TERM REPORTS AGAIN

Yes, envelope-shaking time is here again. We have another batch of mid-term reports. In Letter #3, I explained the significance of the mid-term reports of unsatisfactory work; i.e., "advisory" grades of D and E. In that letter, to demonstrate how mid-term marks are improved by hard work, I showed the proportion of those members of the Class of 1974 whose first mid-term grades improved at the end of the fall term.

The corresponding fall term statistics for '75 are now available. They are quite similar, but I quote them for the record and to serve as another reminder of the improvability of mid-term grades. '75 had a total of 179 unsatisfactory mid-term grades compared to 134 for '74. Sixty-eight per cent of mid-term D's were improved, twelve of them to B's. '75 improved 85% of E-1's to the passing level. The final grade point average for the first term for '75 was 3.56 compared to 3.53 for '74; 32 '75's came up with 5.0 averages compared to 29 for '74, 347 made the Dean's List (4.0 and above) compared with 339 for '74—all told, a pretty fine first term record. For those of you who like to see these things spelled out, here they are:

Mid-Term Grade

	A	B	CP	C−	D	E
D	0	12	29	32	28	6
E-1	0	6	8	15	19	8
E-2	0	1	0	0	1	10
E-3	0	0	0	0	1	3

One always hesitates to generalize concerning the significance of these mid-term reports of unsatisfactory standing, since each one represents an individual case. In November I ventured to suggest that a great majority of those freshmen who were then having academic difficulties were more in need of sympathy, understanding, and encouragement than chiding and exhortation. The first term of college work is challenging, as it should be, and the effort to meet this challenge, while it often involves real struggle, is concomitantly productive of real growth. Numerous aids and services are available to the freshman to help him make his adjustments: it is up to him to take advantage of those which can be helpful to him.

Those of you whose sons had serious difficuties during the first term have by now had opportunity to size up the situation and to appraise your son's response to it, and you therefore can perhaps guess better than we whether your son now needs criticism or encouragement, or both. For those freshmen who had satisfactory grades in the fall term and have one or more unsatisfactory reports at this time, it would perhaps be reasonable in most cases to assume that their present problem is one more of relaxed effort than of deficiencies in preparation or difficulties of the initial adjustment to college life. Such relaxation could be dangerous. On the other hand, it has to be recognized that in a three-course program it can make a significant difference if one or two courses happen to be particularly difficult for a given student. This will be hard for you to appraise: the normal student-to-home report is: "They're all tough." But the fact is that some courses do require more work than others and people differ in what comes hard and what comes easily.

A NOTE ON CAREER AIMS

During the latter half of freshman year, conferences between deans and freshmen frequently get into the question of career aims, since freshmen who are having difficulties, and some of those who are not, frequently suffer from a feeling of lack of direction and motivation. With regard to those goals, I find that in general freshmen can be divided into these four categories:

1. Those who know what they want to do and whose particular aptitudes and talents equip them well for it. This is a happy group, and requires no further comment. (Many of them will change their goals later, but will be just as happy in their revised pursuits.)

2. Those who don't know what they want to do because they have varied abilities and interests; whose problem is selecting what appeals to them most; and who as freshmen are not especially worried about the selection. This is a large group in a liberal arts college, and should be.[1] The men in this group will be discussing careers with their teachers, advisers, parents, and friends; they will consult the Office of Student Services and department chairmen, the deans of our associated schools, and others; they will take care to elect important prerequisite courses which will keep the doors open into the pre-professional courses which they may later select.

3. Those who don't know what they want to do and are worried, depressed, and apologetic about not knowing. For a few of these, their indecision becomes almost a paralyzing obsession. My advice to them is to pick *something* as a tentative goal, in order to feel some sense of direction and purpose; to review and re-examine it periodically (not more often than once a term), utilizing the various advisory resources mentioned above, and the rest of the time to stop worrying about it.

4. Those who think they know what they want to do, but in pursuing it are battering their heads against their weaknesses to their great frustration when with more wisdom they could be going along a different path, along the line of their strengths, with rewards and satisfactions.

It is to the men in this fourth category, and to their parents, that these comments are especially directed. One admires the single-mindedness of their determination; but it is sometimes pathetic to see the frustration, and occasionally the disaster, to which it can

---

1. Relevant quotes: (1) Dartmouth's late President Ernest Martin Hopkins: "The concern of the college is not with what men shall do, but with what they shall be." (2) Woodrow Wilson: "Princeton is not a place where a man goes to find a profession, but a place where he goes to find himself." (3) William Lyon Phelps: "Thank God, I learned nothing useful at Yale College."

lead them. It is most frequently observed in those who are determined to be doctors, when medicine appears quite clearly not to be their dish, considering their particular aptitudes and their grades in college science courses. Every year we watch, sympathetically but helplessly, while a few such men against all the advice offered them here, doggedly pursue these goals right to the brink of suspension from College, or over it. And let's be frank about it: their parents in some cases must bear a large share of the responsibility—more than they usually recognize—because often they are exerting compelling pressures without knowing that they are doing it, or meaning to . . . Not long ago, I heard one experienced college president say, with reference not only to students' career plans: "Many parents act as if they were sending their own egos to college rather than their children."

FRESHMAN FATHERS WEEKEND

The officers of the Freshman Class, with the collaboration of various College officers, are proceeding apace with plans for your Freshman Fathers Weekend, and I am sure that this is going to be another fine occasion: quite possibly, as all hope, the best yet. The attendance prospects seem very gratifying.

I've had a number of letters with regard to conferences with fathers during this weekend. It is quite apparent that, with about 400 fathers in town for 48 hours crowded with events in which you fathers and I and my associate, Dean Manuel, will all be participating, there will be very limited opportunity for private conferences. In the circumstances, it seems best to try to handle these as well as we can on a catch-as-catch-can basis, without undertaking to make definite appointments at particular times. There will be a limited opportunity on Saturday morning of the weekend for such conferences and Dean Manuel and I will be available on Sunday for others.

Let me share with you a letter shared with me at this season in a recent year by a southern parent. The names are fictitious. "Hal" is an older brother who was then a Dartmouth senior:

Hello—

I've got to get out of this place! The skiing was really great Fri., but it's starting to get slushy again, and it's truly miserable. Hal isn't having a date either this weekend, so we're thinking about going skiing somewhere.

There's just nothing to write about. Except for the skiing this place is really terrible. Crew is no fun, and I don't want to do it anyway, so I'll probably drop it. Hal will get mad and so will you, but if I don't want to do it, it's a waste of my time even though I would get some great physical benefits from it. I hate cold weather.

I really hate this place. It's just not the place for me at all. If I can stick it out this year, I think I will try to get a leave of absence and join the Army, and then try it again in a few years. If I survive Vietnam, maybe I can make another start and by then I will be ready for it.

I just cannot study here. My mind will just not take it in and I can't concentrate, so I end up not studying nearly what I ought to, and I'm going to burn badly in the grades department.

There's really nothing to report. Carnival will be terrible, the weather is terrible, the books are terrible, the food is terrible, I'm not sleeping well, and the whole world seems totally worthless.

       Good-bye
       Rich

P.S. Please disregard everything I've said (except about crew). I really had nothing to write about, so I wrote a sample letter from a freshman in the throes of the winter-wish-I-was-any-where-but-here syndrome. Now you can give Mom the smelling salts, Dad.

Many thanks for your recent letters, which indicate that the symptoms of the first college vacation and of the January return haven't changed much.

Sincerely yours,
ALBERT I. DICKERSON

P.S. I enclose for your information a new pamphlet on the Dartmouth Plan which has just become available.

Parents Letter #6

March 24, 1972

Dear Parents of '75:

"SPRING IS HERE TO STAY," Gimbel's is wont to say in large type in the *New York Times* at just about this time of year. This is nonsense, of course, as anyone in these parts could tell you. Spring will come and go for some time here. For a few days it will be warm and sunny. The snow will melt and the sap will run in the maples. Then it will snow again. Then nearby Lebanon, registering a temperature some notches below zero, will be advertised as "the coldest spot in the nation." Then will come windy stretches when all is gray and raw . . . So we run, it seems endlessly, through the cycle: snow, ice, sun, mud; snow, ice, sun, mud . . .

You can see I'm working up to the description of another syndrome: the Schlump Syndrome. Schlump is the local name for this season of the Hanover year.

WINTER TERM GRADE REPORTS

But first, we must get on to the business of this letter, or at least the excuse for it: the transmission of the enclosed winter term grade reports. I guess, now that you have become veterans in grade-receiving, little comment is needed. Since the '75's are all over everywhere, they will receive their copies of the grade reports upon their return; so if they're with you, please share your copies with them. There will be some happy surprises and inevitably a number of unhappy ones, too. The figures will certainly be very similar to those of recent classes for the winter term, which means that something like two dozen men will get perfect 5.0's. About 25% of the class will get 4.3 or better. About 35% will get 4.0 or better. The breakpoints between quarters will come in the 4.0, the 3.7, and the 3.0 groups, which means that every 4.0 man is entitled to consider himself in the top quarter, 3.7 in the top half, and 3.0 in the top three-fourths. The class average for the term will be something above 3.0 (it was 3.56 for '74). Nobody has yet been ingenious enough to contrive a class without a lowest quarter, no matter how good the class may be; so inevitably some 200 '75's will be there. Some of these will graduate *summa cum laude*.

THE SCHLUMP SYNDROME

Now for a look at the Schlump (or "Let's-Get-the-Heck-Out-of-Here") Syndrome mostly for fun... The symptoms begin to appear in the latter half of February. It is then that the term's second flurry of hour exams occurs, term papers come due, the spectre of finals begins to loom over the horizon, and the end-of-term pressures begin to build up. For some reason these pressures are more apparent during the winter term than during the fall, possibly because they are accentuated by the onset of schlump.

Here let's digress a moment from schlump to identify some differences between the troubled ones of the winter term and those of the fall term, differences which have nothing to do with weather. Let's take Hal Ramsey,[1] as a characteristic example of winter term discouragement. Hal, like so many, is a serious and highly motivated student. Like so many, he got high grades in high school. Like so many, he had rough sledding in the fall term. However, people had told him that it would be like this and so he wasn't unduly discouraged. He wound up that term with a 1.7 and an academic warning, so he buckled down to work even harder during the winter. He gave up all of the fun things, cut out the last bits of time-wasting,

1. Ramsey, Beston, Armstrong and Sanders are fictitious names, but the cases are from Real Life.

and booked and booked. He was interested in his courses. But again, at winter mid-term he found himself with a D and an E. By this time he was pretty depressed. His letters home became increasingly despondent. He was taking reading and study skills programs and learning useful things, but would he master these in time to be saved? He had clutched in a fall-term French final. Would he do it again? He was doing everything that he could to succeed. What could a dean tell him? Not much more than to be of good heart, keep trying, relax, have a little fun, get enough sleep and exercise, and be confident that his combination of high motivation, interest in his work, more than adequate abilities, and developing experience with college work would result, sooner or later, in higher grades . . . Hal is typical of a great many of the troubled people of the winter term. Most of those in Hal's category will begin to find their rewards in the spring term.

Now let's return to the Schlump Syndrome, whose phenomenology is very similar to that previously described for the January Wish-I-Were-Somewhere-Else Syndrome. Its peculiar characteristic is its contagiousness. It spreads through roommates, corridors, dormitories. It has a curious way of infecting students who come from the same schools or home towns. Take, as an example of the galloping contagion of this odd affliction, the Beston Case. Leslie Beston (pseudonym) came from a suburb north of Chicago. Although his was a January case, his symptoms differed from those of the January Syndrome, whose sufferers by and large are afflicted by the normal frustrations of the freshman struggle for academic and social recognition. Beston had earned a fall-term 3.7 (which then put him in the top quarter) while being a prominent member of the freshman football team. He had won considerable recognition. But, he said, he had to work so hard doing it that life just wasn't worth the candle. So off he went in January to a mid-western university "where you don't have to work so hard"—(and where there are GIRLS).

Come Schlump that year, we began to run into a series of cases of this special virus, which we began to trace back to Beston. Eventual research proved that a large number of these sufferers had been infected by a non-filterable, itchy virus which became known as the "Beston Strain." The geographical origins of the sufferers showed a heavy concentration around Chicago, and it was eventually found that the infection had raged through the North Shore suburbs all the way to Palatine. (Practically all recovered.)[2] Such infections have also been found to spread from campus to campus: certain restless strains have been traced to New Haven, Williamstown, Cambridge, and elsewhere, and it was later reported that the Beston Strain had infected some of his friends at Williams and Yale.

Another example of the curious communicability of the Schlump Syndrome comes to mind. John Armstrong and George Sanders attended the same country day school in, say, Pennsylvania. On February 27 in that year, John Armstrong came in. He had been looking into the University of Accra in Ghana. He was going home that weekend and wanted to discuss a leave of absence next year, to be spent probably in Ghana . . . Late in the afternoon of the same day, George Sanders came in. He'd been looking into the Army's six-month deal and was considering a leave of absence for military service. He also let drop the fact that he had given some thought to the University of Accra in Ghana . . . Accra twice in the same day. And the Hillcrest Country Day School. One couldn't help putting 2 and 2 together. Here were two young men not rooming together, not especially close friends, both doing well academically, both intellectually curious and interested in their courses, both appearing to have outside interests and satisfactory circles of friends and not the slightest indication of (if you'll pardon the expression) poor "adjustment."

2. Beston also recovered. His letters from Mid-West U. during the ensuing months become more and more nostalgic, and the following January he rejoined his class in Hanover, where, as everybody knows, everybody WORKS HARD and GIRLS are few. His letter of application for readmission is worth quoting. "I left Dartmouth last year saying that the reason I was leaving was because I disliked Dartmouth. But now I realize that what I did dislike about Dartmouth was that it was trying to make a man out of the high school boy I was. I was not ready for this remodeling, and I decided to leave. Now I regret that immature decision, and I sincerely wish that I will be able to gain readmittance into Dartmouth." He did, and graduated in the top 6th of his class after captaining wrestling and enjoying a lot of rugby.

Armstrong (he who discovered Ghana's University of Accra) was in again just before the spring recess. He was now thinking about military service . . . And how about Sanders? Well, you've guessed it. Sanders was now gung-ho about Ghana.

Throughout the spring term, the Armstrong-Sanders strain kept cropping up among their acquaintances. This was unusual, since there aren't many spring syndromes. Withdrawal symptoms tend to disappear as the elms begin to bud.[3]

So you will begin to get the picture of the Schlump Syndrome. I shall now come clean and admit that I have purposely concealed, up to now, the symptomatology of Schlump. I try, in general, to top you off in advance to the up-and-down curves of freshman morale. But the comunicability of the Schlump Syndrome has held me back for fear of increasing the incidence of these diseases simply by talking about them.

Any catalogue of syndromes should include the California Syndrome. Sufferers from this syndrome don't really suffer—often they are very happy at Dartmouth. It's just that, after a while, continued separation from that Garden of Eden on the west coast seems hardly endurable. Similar symptom patterns are sometimes observed in Texans.

Considering the variety of afflictions to which undergraduates are susceptible—including academic catastrophe and severe illness—it is perhaps surprising and reassuring that 787 of the 811 '75's who arrived in September are, as of this writing, still on board.

MARCH IN HANOVER

One of the minor triumphs of Dartmouth's unique academic calendar is that it manages to eliminate from the academic year one-half

---

3. Sanders remained, played lacrosse, sang in the glee club, made a late shift into a math major (which "ain't easy to do"), and graduated with his class. Armstrong? He never got to Accra but did get, successively, to the universities of Perugia and Madrid, returned after a year, took a brief fling toward chemical engineering, changed to a Spanish major, got 4.5 his last two terms, was admitted to a distinguished university to work for a Ph.D. in Spanish, and later took a job on the Dartmouth faculty.

of the month of March. March is, let's face it, in New England, *awful*. Our job in this office is to understand and minister to the sufferings of freshmen. We do this with earnest dedication throughout the season of schlump. But last week, as we talked with departing freshmen who, relaxed after finals, headed for their homes (almost all of which are south of here), or Florida, or Nassau, or even skiing in Europe, or other generally southerly destinations, let us confess to feeling more envy than empathy.

Many of your sons are with you as this is written, although some may have left before it arrives and some did not come home. Some of them are now here in Hanover. So many, in fact, that three dormitories had to be opened for them. About 185 students (including 53 freshmen) signed up for rooms with the avowed intention of spending some days here. A score or so of freshmen signed for the "entire" recess, but from previous experience in trying to reach students during the recess, one knows that these plans are lavishly subject to change.

One wonders about the proportion of booking, the avowed purpose for most, to other pursuits. At the moment, Baker Library is not what could be called congested. But would not one say that a student should have a chance to discover the qualities of corn snow, to learn the capacity of the March sun to impart a ruddy glow, to tramp the spongy roads back in the hills, and, if it's his first New England spring, to sample the sweetish stuff in the roadside sap buckets as a thirst-quencher? If by nightfall he is a bit too drowsy for productive scholarship, well, tomorrow it may rain. (Anybody for bridge?) If there *are* many students in Hanover, they are not highly visible: a leisurely pair here and there on the sidewalks, unencumbered by books or visible concerns, and a few wandering in and out of the Main Street eateries at the odd hours at which undergraduates wander in and out of eateries.

To those whose sons aren't with you and may be here, may I say that I know how you've missed them. I also know, as one who came to college here at some distance from home and spent several college vacations in Hanover, your son has not had a bad time. Hanover is a nice town, and never more so than during a recess when, very suddenly, it ceases being a teeming educational enterprise and becomes for the nonce a little New England village. No Dartmouth student who fails to stay here long enough in some vacation period (yes, even in March) to find this out has had the full Dartmouth experience. (You should try it yourself sometime.)

ON BRINGING FRIENDS HOME

It is a time-honored tradition of collegiate vacationing, especially if one feels himself in danger of parental admonition over grades or something, to bring a friend home—usually a friend with lower grades and, in these days, longer hair and wilder beard. This is an application of the Buffer Principle, and usually brings into operation the Reinforcement Ploy. Both are part of the broad strategy of dinner table defense, based on the axiom that 97.6% of parent-son holiday contact is at the dinner table. The Buffer Principle is a concept of defense in depth. (If your son brought *two* guests home for the holidays, you'd better stop right now and examine the enclosed grade report.) The B.P. assumes that a parent could hardly be so graceless, with guests present, as to intrude persistent questions of a tactless or depressing nature into the gaiety of dinner conversation. The Reinforcement Ploy is the second line of defense, against the possibility of an awkward breakthrough. It goes something like this:

Father: I noticed that mid-term E-2 in math . . .
Son: Gosh, Dad, I've been meaning to tell you. I really got dinged in that course. Isn't that so, Joe?
Guest: Yes, gee, Mr. Abercrombie. That's the toughest course . . .
Son: And Professor Whittleby is the toughest marker in Dartmouth. Everybody says so. Isn't that right, Joe?
Guest: Yes, Sir, Mr. Abercrombie. He grades on the curve, and the way he curves it, guys who get Whittleby's D's would get B's from Professor Grindstone. Isn't that so, Jack?

Son: It sure is, Joe. You remember Len (he's the guy down the hall, Dad...). (Long story about Len who hardly ever booked and got one of Grindstone's B's.)

Guest: Yes, Sir, Mr. Abercrombie, and I want you to know how hard Jack's booked ever since Carnival. He was in the library all the time . . .

Son: That was the toughest final I ever saw, Dad. I just missed a D by two points and if I hadn't misread those last three questions, I'd have C-Mined it easy . . . (Telephone rings. Tactical retreat from table accomplished with practiced speed. Sound of car going out driveway.)

If your son is home, with or without guests, how are things, compared with Christmas? A little more assurance? A little less assertiveness? Are things veering around, so that you find that now *you*, and *your* foibles and odd notions, are getting the Tolerant Treatment? One thing is certain. Your vocabulary has grown. You now know all about loose-hanging and booking. If your son is lucky, you've learned about "Ace-ing" exams. Perhaps the image of "floaters" and "screamers" and "flamers," and other peculiar specimens which inhabit college dormitories will have begun to come into a sort of dim focus.

LEVELING OFF

Yielding to the always dangerous temptation to generalize, I frequently think of the fall term as the adjustment term, the winter term as the shake-down term, and the spring term as the leveling-off term. For most of those who had fall-term difficulties, the winter "shake-down" has meant "settling in," getting organized and learning the knacks of college study. Now we find these men out of the woods. For a dozen or so of the immature and unmotivated, "shake-down" will mean a "shake out," this term or next.

In some cases the winter term resembles a deferred "adjustment term" or a premature "sophomore slump." I think of a freshman of this category who, after a good first term, had a bad winter term. "To my great surprise," he said, "I found work last term not difficult at all, so I decided that college wasn't so tough after all. I started taking things easy this term. Now I've learned my lesson."

Then there is the pattern of underachievery, whose practitioners live cheerfully on the edges of disaster, sometimes fall over the brink, frequently don't. Occasionally they get belatedly fired with ambition and go places, having left behind in their days of underachievery a wake of futilely exhorting parents, deans, counselors and friends. More often, unfortunately, they continue to thread their ways along the soft shoulders of the byways where warnings, probations, and suspensions lurk; and fall by the wayside during the sophomore year, the period of greatest attrition in the undergraduate years.

The "leveling-off" pattern of the spring term means "leveling-off-upwards" in the normal case. The typical student from this point on follows a gradual climb in grades, with minor peaks and valleys. The occasional one climbs sharply to distinction. A few loose-hangers "level off downward," drift into sophomore year, get suspended or withdraw for "lack of motivation"—and in a large percentage of cases, return later after some kind of growing-up experience to do a real job.

We are mindful of the group of men like Hal Ramsey who begin the third term still feeling somewhat depressed and discouraged that so much work during the preceding two terms has not produced more rewards in terms of grades. Sometimes for these men in the early weeks of the new term, things seem not to be starting off much more encouragingly than before. But for most of them, as the spring weeks move on, the usual rewards of industry and dedication begin to appear as, finally, they develop the ability to organize their time and as they acquire the knacks of college study which are the major achievements of freshman year for most.

And one mustn't forget, having spent relatively little time with them, that sizeable group who start strong, continue strong, and finish strong.

So, for all of us, spring eventually *does* come. The spring term is the golden term. Owing to the vagaries of the calendar, it is usually the shortest of the three terms, requiring the compression of the courses by 5 to 10 per cent. It always seems to go very fast.

I am happy to announce that our team has a new member: Britta S. McNemar, Assistant Dean of the College for the past two years, has moved across the hall as Assistant Dean of Freshmen to help us get through the rest of this year while getting ready for next year, when we will have 1000 freshmen, including close to 200 coeds for the first time in Dartmouth's 202 years. Dean McNemar will work interchangeably with Dean Manuel and me in all aspects of the work of this office. She will continue as Dean in Choate Residence, where she and her husband, Professor Donald W. McNemar of the Department of Government, reside. A native of Pittsburgh, she is a graduate of Connecticut College and holds a Master's degree from the University of Pennsylvania. At Dartmouth, while serving in Dean Brewster's office, she has been coordinator of the 12-College Exchange Program. She has served on several important committees, including the Committee on Year Round Operation, which devised the Dartmouth Plan and implemented coeducation, and the recent long-range planning committee for student residence.

This letter carries the best wishes of all of us for the wind-up freshman term of '75.

Sincerely yours,
ALBERT I. DICKERSON

P.S. In case there is any uncertainty about the registration date of spring term, it is Tuesday, March 28, from 1:30 to 4:30 p.m. and 7:00 to 10:00 p.m.

14. Dean Dickerson receiving from President John G. Kemeny, at the first meeting of the freshman class in the fall of 1970, a gift marking the 40th anniversary of his appointment to the Dartmouth administrative staff. Below: He talks with Dean of the College Carroll W. Brewster at the 1970 Convocation.

Parents Letter #7

May 11, 1972

Dear Friends:

Two or three pretty days within the past week intimate that spring is eventually about to reach us, even though some heaps of dirty snow under the north eaves of the Alumni Gymnasium are still with us.

The freshman year of the Class of 1975 is rushing down the homestretch with the usual speed—a fact which your sons comment upon as we see them these days.

We now have the mid-term reports for this term ready to go to you as your last set of such reports as a Dartmouth parent. Therefore, unless you have younger sons or daughters coming along, this is the end of your envelope-shaking career.

Previous letters in this series (#3 and #5) have dwelt enough on the nature of these reports and you have had enough statistical evidence of the improvability of mid-term D's and E's. The majority of the 15 who are on probation this term seem to be working themselves out of the woods, although in somewhat lower proportion than usual.

As I look back at this time of year on this series of Parents Letters, I have the feeling that they have been unduly preoccupied with problems and worries, in the effort to put the former in perspective, to allay the latter, and to dissipate the numerous anxieties which have no real foundation at all. We have joked in previous letters about your sons' reports of high endeavor and cerebral derring-do, but these freshmen *have* worked. And they've grown. We see it every day in talking to men whom we have seen earlier in the year.

We usually manage to invite most of the freshmen in during the year for conferences on their progress and plans—except for those we have talked with during the year in the Dining Hall, Dick's House, or elsewhere outside the office. Normally, all but a few dozen get in before the June finals. And normally, the freshmen one meets in May tend to be a happy lot. If they have had problems earlier, they have usually solved them by now; and if they have had their worries or discontents, by this time these have gone away. The May freshman is a maturer and more confident fellow than the October freshman—more confident but at the same time having more humility; more critical and at the same time more tolerant; more aware; and we think, a little wiser. He is interested in his work and looking ahead, often with impressive resourcefulness and foresight. He has struck out into one or more extra-classroom enterprises.

I don't know how familiar you are with the geography of Hanover. Just behind our office is Massachusetts Lane, which runs along the Massachusetts row of dormitories to Thayer Hall; and we park our cars in an area behind the Massachusetts Row dormitories. In the morning and at noon and frequently in the evening, we meet students on the way to and from their meals in Thayer. In the morning they're in a hurry, and travel in ones and twos, frequently on the run. The other times at this season they are in leisurely groups. The groups get bigger as the year wears on, from the fall when they travel briskly in pairs in animated conversations about Camus, to the spring when they move in squads and platoons, often with horseplay. The springtime pace is one of confidence and ease. Among the groups one may spot a gaily clowning character who was in the office last winter talking somberly about transferring to Harvard or Pomona, or to Hometown U. near family and/or girl. The individuals are large and small, introverted and extroverted, gay and sober, natty and sloppy, shaven and stubbled; long-haired and short-haired and "medium"; sometimes mustached and/or bearded, and frequently side-burned to the jowls. There is a great variety here, which does not fit into anyone's stereotype of the "college boy." But watching these groups in the perspective of these closing weeks of the term, one gets a renewed sense not only of the wonderful diversity of Dartmouth undergraduates but also of the pervasive *quality* of a Dartmouth class as it is about to move into its upperclass years.

In the last Parents Letter I predicted that "something like two dozen" would get 5.0's and 55 men came through with such records. Some of these were aided by the use of the Non-Recording Option (popularly known as "pass-fail") in one of their courses: the number of men who got a perfect set of three A's (48) was a little nearer the prediction. I forecast that about 25% of the class would get 4.3 or better and actually 242 (30%) did so. It was predicted that about 35% would produce records of 4.0 or better and actually 363 (45%) men produced such records. The class average for the term was predicted at around 3.0 and it was 3.64 compared with 3.56 for the Class of 1974 during the winter term. A steady rise in grade point averages has been observed here and elsewhere over recent years, and there has been some speculation about the factors producing this gradual inflation; but nevertheless, these figures reflect a solid performance by the Class of 1975.

At this point, I think a specific word of appreciation to the parents of '75 is in order. At the beginning of the year, I ventured to suggest that it does not help a worried boy if he has to shoulder the burden of his parents' anxieties on top of his own. As I look back now on the year to date, I am struck with the strong impression that you have given thoughtful and sensitive attention to this suggestion, and that the '75 freshmen have enjoyed the opportunity to work out their own problems—as in the last analysis they must do—with the help of your understanding, encouragement, forbearance, and confidence.

It may be that I'll add a message to accompany the final grades for the term, but if so, it will do no harm to say these appreciative words twice.

Sincerely yours,
ALBERT I. DICKERSON

7. Miscellany

Never Say Diet by Corey Ford*

"This slight volume" may not be, in the lexicon of writers and publishers, a happy augury in the opening sentence of book reviews. It is, however, the proper accolade for this book which is easy to pick up, easy to put down, easy to raise and lower fifty times from the standing, sitting, prone, or fifth-martini position—and is on the subject of Diet.

Mr. Ford obviously enjoyed writing it, Mr. Taylor clearly convulsed himself doing the drawings, you will share their sensations in reading it—and the only dark ambivalence in this whole rollicking picture is the "why-do-you-suppose-the-Book-Review-Editor-thought-of-me?" speculation of the reviewer.

This frivolous introduction should not lead the prospective reader to think that this opus, however low its specific gravity, lacks Substance and Truth. There is more than a little of universality in it. Who of us, soon or late, by the iron whim of spouse, mother, aunt or Solicitous Friend, or his own passing masochistic impulse has not come under the flesh-mortifying discipline of Dr. Hausrecker's regimen of wheat-germ, yogurt, and that dark destroyer, black strap molasses—or Dr. X's version of last or next year, which is totally new in every respect other than its totally repulsive quality. Here, then, is the delirious vision of liberation, reaching its climax in Chapter 6—the Live Older, Look Longer Diet Plan of Dr. Schlump. ("Do You Want To Live A Hundred Years On Yogurt?")

We won't tell you how this book comes out. However, a word about the author and illustrator. Dr. Ford, who signs himself "Department of Lipophilics, Dartmouth College," has a shadowy

*A book review written in 1954.

connection with Dartmouth's alumni body as president, secretary, treasurer, class agent and sole member of the Class of 19--, and occasionally publishes letters from himself in the classnotes section of the *Alumni Magazine* (and will someday no doubt salute his own memory in some magnificent obituary) and locally is more familiarly and muscularly known as proprietor of Corey Ford's Gymnasium on North Balch Street. Mr. Taylor, the *New Yorker* artist who is in his own beguiling fashion even more macabre than Chas. Addams, is the perfect, the ineluctable illustrator of this volume. Even his characters' eyeballs are corpulent—including the more skeletal ones like the sad, bearded, bony ascetic in this volume who graces one of the flyleaves among the book's 25 forewords, prefaces, prologues and introductions, over the title: "All you have to do is avoid certain things that are fattening, such as food."

The one sad thought we have about *Never Say Diet* concerns the limitations on its readership. It would seem a natural for the Hostess Present Market—cheaper than chocolates, zinnias, or smoking tobacco; more likely to get opened than, say *Le Temps Retrouvé*; and easy to wrap, mail or slip in the suitcase. But it would be a reckless guest who would risk it except on (1) the Naturally Thin Woman (i.e. not (a) the Secret Dieter or (b) the Unhappy Ulceree) and (2) the gay pigeon with whom he had sneaked out to the kitchen for a surreptitious nightcap of whipped cream and apple pie. If Messrs. Ford and Taylor were depending heavily on this book's market for hostesses for their 1954–55 groceries they can just throw away Dr. Schlump's Calorie Counter, ingenious as it is, and forget about the whole grim, ghastly business.

ALBERT I. DICKERSON '30

Open Letter to the New Hampshire House of Representatives

As a resident of a friendly neighboring state, living close by the New Hampshire border and interested in education, I have followed with admiration your imaginative deliberations during this session concerning the problems of state finance and the furtherance of education in New Hampshire at all levels. My observation of your activities, it might be added, is somewhat wistful and nostalgic, since I once lived in New Hampshire and moved out—no farther than necessary!—because property taxes made home-owning expensive in New Hampshire. I have been especially impressed by the conceptions recently advanced for "lotteries" and "sweepstakes."

One cannot help being struck—particularly at this time when we residents of less forward-looking states are doing our income tax returns—by the kind of vision credited to Alderman John McDonough of Manchester for his lottery bill. The potential benefits of this legislation to schools in New Hampshire—to use his own words as quoted in the *Boston Herald* on March 6—"stagger the imagination."

My hat is off to you Ladies and Gentlemen of the General Court who have had the courage to reject the arguments of self-righteous people who still talk tritely about Sin Taxes. The benefits of these taxes have been eloquently described in the Legislature many times. However, there is a corollary value to these taxes which, it seems to me, has never been adequately recognized: the feeling of moral uplift, as a participant in the great cause of furthering New Hampshire education, which these taxes offer to so many people including even visitors from other states.

The customer who walks out of the state store carries with him not only his bottle but a warm glow—the glow of satisfaction that comes from knowing he has just helped the third graders at Henniker get a better blackboard. Walking away from the vending machine, the smoker quickly dispels his nagging speculation about the state of his lungs with the happy thought that he has just supported the teaching of French in Franconia. One should not underestimate the impacts of all these little actions on the moral values and satisfactions of all the smoking and drinking citizenry, doing their part in a great cause.

Then there is Rockingham. I've never been there, but this isn't because I haven't wanted to. I'm determined to get over there this year: not only for the pleasant drive, the fresh air, and the fun of watching the horses, but because I know that even one $2 bet would help New Hampshire to educate its young people. Consider the man from Methuen who gets there often: in one afternoon, making only two stops, he can help the State of New Hampshire through purchases of cigarettes, gasoline and liquor (he judiciously does these errands on the way *in*) and can then go home, after enjoying the horses and the fresh air, realizing that he has helped to educate his friends' children in Salem, even if he has blown his family's groceries for the following week.

Indeed, Ladies and Gentlemen, I would not only agree that this talk about Sin Taxes is nonsense, but I would respectfully suggest that we have not begun to go far enough with "Sin."

For one thing, New Hampshire needs at least one or two educational dog tracks. What, for example, is wrong with Durham for dog racing? It is near enough to Maine and Massachusetts to appeal to friends of New Hampshire education in those states. The State owns facilities in Durham which could be converted at small expense for dog track use, with only minor inconvenience to the University's athletic program—small in comparison with the many great benefits which would be reaped. Think of these benefits. Thousands of additional dollars to be poured into education all over the State. The University's athletic teams could use the facilities when they were not in use by the dogs. The students would have a wholesome new outdoor entertainment for many of their afternoons and evenings in good weather. The influx of visitors would be educational in itself. Durham merchants would prosper. Mathematics students would learn more about probability than they do in the classroom, and if they guessed right, could lighten their families' financial burdens. The dogs would be a stimulus to veterinary education. Etc., etc.

New Hampshire opponents of more adequate racing facilities are, in my view, short-sighted and reactionary in the extreme. The fact that racing has led to widespread corruption in high and low places elsewhere certainly does *not* mean this could happen in New Hampshire. (Even my own state is moving forward in exploring the educational benefits of racing.)

The lotteries are an obvious next step for the benefit of those who can't conveniently get to the tracks, even if, hopefully, we get more adequate racing facilities. Let me simply urge that you legislators with vision resist stoutly any pernicious efforts to write restrictive legislation on the prospective distribution of lottery tickets. There is, of course, an obvious convenience and economy in the proposed use of liquor stores for distribution of lottery tickets. However, it is indispensable that we find some way to serve the needs of the Soda Fountain Set and their desire to support good educational causes. Under current law, only those who have reached 21 may patronize the state stores. Until that law is revised —as it should be down to, say, 16—the problem of giving our young people a chance to serve might be solved by providing all of the state's licensed pharmacists with licenses as lottery ticket distributors, also. This would serve to bring opportunity within reach of the soda fountain.

One cannot help thinking of the thousands of boys and girls who come in from other states to our schools and colleges, who are under 21 and want to help. Consider the impact which this enterprising and imaginative legislation will have outside New Hampshire's borders; and the strength that will surely accrue to New Hampshire's educational enterprises from this national awareness of New Hampshire's imaginative approach to educational needs. There are numerous educational institutions in New Hampshire which, in total, bring in thousands of students from other states. Spreading the news of New Hampshire's new statewide educational enterprises through all these families dispersed all over the United States cannot help but have beneficial effects on the state.

With the administrative mechanism established, statewide, for lotteries, it would be the height of fiscal imprudence not to use these facilities for operation of "off-the-track" betting on racing. This, I'm sure, is already in your planning.

Now finally, Ladies and Gentlemen of the General Court, after these observations of praise and these few suggestions of minor import, I come respectfully to my only proposal that has real Scope.

It is not, really, a very original idea; and I cannot imagine how it has been overlooked all this time. Perhaps it hasn't, and in my rather spotty reading of New Hampshire educational journals I just missed it.

A few paragraphs back I subscribed to your own apparent conviction that New Hampshire hasn't yet begun to go far enough along with what the stuffily-minded refer to as "Sin." We have, indeed, overlooked the most fruitful, ageless, and broadly-embracing area of them all. Historically, it antedates by many centuries such time-honored innovations as racing and gambling. Possibly it may even antedate drinking. It might be said that it goes all the way back to Adam. How could we have missed it?

Its introduction as an activity conducted under the sovereign auspices of the State of New Hampshire would surely bring the Golden Age to New Hampshire education. And it would be so simple to organize and administer. All that would be necessary would be to add a second storey to all the New Hampshire liquor stores. Thus you would neatly have all of New Hampshire's officially recognized and licensed sins efficiently organized under one roof, in the service of New Hampshire education.

Let me recall my earlier reference to the moral uplift inherent in New Hampshire's tax structure even in the present day, and the warm glow of New Hampshire's benefactor of education as he emerges with his bottle from the state store. Try to picture the ambient effulgence of next year's customer as he goes out that front door . . . carrying with him his bottle, his lottery ticket, and his bet on the 6th race at Rockingham.

         Respectfully yours,
         A WISTFUL EXPATRIATE

March 1963

Remarks in Acknowledgment of the Gift to Dartmouth College of a Portrait of Sidney Chandler Hayward, Class of 1926, Secretary of the College

Drake Room, Hopkins Center, March 22, 1963

Whatever the Scriptures may say about the relative blessedness of giving and receiving, I feel extraordinarily blessed today to stand here as the symbolic recipient: speaking, with due authorization, in the name of the College.

Thus, in expressing thanks for this portrait, which from this moment becomes a prized possession of this institution, I speak not merely for all those who are here—save Sid Hayward himself—but for that immeasurable entity which is respected and loved by us here, and by so many others spread around this planet: Dartmouth College.

The opportunity to speak in this name is one not lightly taken. I have three packages of thanks to deliver.

First, our thanks to the donors who have conceived and underwritten this so appropriate gift to Dartmouth and this so richly merited tribute to Sid Hayward. There are twenty-one names on this list. The only reason that there are not more is that nobody else was invited. There could easily have been twenty-one thousand.

Second, to the artist who has given us this splendid portrait, Peter Michael Gish, Class of 1949. He has brought to it not only his fine artistry, but also the *feeling* that we, Sid's friends and admirers, would wish it to reflect. It has been painted with warmth and affection and respect. We thank you, Peter Gish.

Third, and most importantly, Dartmouth's thanks go to the man who has provided the reason for it all.

Sid, you have conceived, planned, organized, and conducted so many great occasions—some very large; some small, but also great,

15. Dean Dickerson as public speaker. Top: accepting the gift to the College of a portrait of Sidney C. Hayward '26, Secretary of the College, in 1963. Below: speaking at Freshman Fathers Weekend in February 1970.

like this one. You're the "old pro" at doing things like this the right way. It is understandable if you are uneasy about being yourself in the spotlight with someone else at the rheostat. When you're in charge, you never let things get too solemn. We pledge you that we shall not, either.

My credentials as a spokesman are fairly good in terms of length of observation. A few here may have watched Sid Hayward, at work and at play, for longer than I. But not many.

The label on the portrait says "Secretary of the College 1930– ." We thank heaven for the blank space. To be personal, I believe it was on almost this same date in 1930, thirty-three years ago, when you, Sid, and Bob Strong, invited me up to luncheon in order to decide whether Mr. Hopkins should hire me to take over some of the jobs which you relinquished when you became Secretary of the College. As I remember it, it was a very bright day, like this one. I'm so glad you made the right decision.

This is not the occasion for a recital of all that Sid Hayward has done for Dartmouth, and all that he has meant to his friends, through all of these years. Let us just leave it at this, and leave it in the form of a question: Who can think of another who can match these Hayward years: who can match these years in dedication to Dartmouth, or in warmth, or in resourcefulness, or in vigor, or in imagination, or in humor . . . and, along with all these things, in numbers, too?

So in the end, Sid, we come to thanking YOU for this: for what it signifies here today to us, and for what it will signify through the years to Dartmouth.

1930 Testimonial Dinner for Eddie Jeremiah
Boston, April 4, 1966

Mr. President, Ladies and Gentlemen, and
Dear Former Friend:

I am sure everyone in this room regards himself as being one of Jerry's long-time cherished friends, with the possible exception of the waiters and, sad to say, the definite exception of myself. I hasten to reassure you, Mr. President, that I do not intend to introduce a discordant note in this evening's laudatory proceedings. I spent 20 happy years in the warm fellowship of the friends of Jeremiah, and my departure from that fraternity has not affected my admiration for our distinguished classmate and your beloved friend.

One of the many fine qualities of Jerry's which have been and will be alluded to tonight is a certain quality of candor and directness. Soon after he came back to Hanover to coach in 1937, he revealed to Bob Strong, then director of admissions, that his ultimate goal was to be a combination hockey coach and director of admissions. Jerry, however, is not one to pull out his goalie in the first period; so with that patience, which is another fine quality that Jerry practices, when necessary, he started his admissions career quietly, in the role of part-time adviser, consultant, and helper.

Bob Strong died with tragic suddenness in 1946 at the age of 46—a wonderful person to whom Jerry, among others, has paid touching tribute. The president and trustees were faced with the unexpected problem of finding a replacement. Jerry hadn't gotten around to letting John Dickey know about his long-range plans. So I wound up in the admissions hotseat, instead.

Here another of the great Jeremiah qualities came to the fore—his magnanimity. Did Jerry let it rankle that after all of his on-the-job training some rank outsider had copped the plum? No, indeed. He just started out helping *me*. By definition, the prime qualification of the great coach is being a good teacher. Jerry is a great teacher. Admissions people keep talking about things like rank-in-class, verbal aptitude, mathematical aptitude. Jerry pointed out that this was a very limited way to look at the promise of college candidates. It left out of account a lot of other aptitudes. For one example, skating; for another, stick-handling. I should carry the message back to the College Board: there were grave omissions in their test battery. "You guys in the Admissions Office go at everything the wrong way," he said. "The first thing you ask for on Form 1 is a photograph. What kind of photograph do you ask for? 'Head and shoulders.' Why, you can't even tell whether he's wearing skates."

That spring when, beleaguered and bedraggled, I had alienated most of my friends and God knows how many potential benefactors of the College, who but Jerry in all his generosity could offer consolation: "I will nominate you for rookie of the year," he said.

Those were the years of the Rileys. As long as the Riley family kept sending sons to Dartmouth, it didn't really matter much to Jerry how many stupid mistakes the admissions office made on promising skaters and stickhandlers from Melrose and Minnesota. But at last came the night when the last Riley played his last game for Dartmouth. After that game, it is reliably reported, Jerry accosted Mr. Riley and said: "You cad: you quit on me too soon."

In the post-Riley period, Jerry's tutelage as admissions adviser became more intensive. Ultimately, alas, he grew disappointed with me as a pupil. There were those times when the skating aptitude seemed to have an inverse relationship to the verbal aptitude; and, if the College Board had an instrument for measuring stickhandling, it would have been 800 when the candidate's mathematical aptitude was 300.

Jerry's big heart, as you would expect, carried us through these times. He spoke to me on the street. In the proper season—spring or summer, that is—he could make a good Jeremiah joke. I would wander too close to Jerry's dugout at a freshman baseball game. His pitcher would be in tight control, his hitters blasting the pastures, the score nine to nothing, and I would hear a very audible, familiar voice, saying sadly: "Well, this is what the admissions office gives us, but we do the best that we can." . . . Ralph Manuel '58,* a nice young guy in the admissions office who played baseball under Jerry, was watching Jerry knock out grounders to his infielders. The third baseman muffed three chances in a row. Jerry leaned on his bat after the third one and called to Ralph: "He's not a very good glove-man, but he's got a 700 Verbal." But my letters from Jerry began to open with the salutation: "Dear Former Friend."

Those were the post-Riley hard times of those warm winters, when Jerry phrased immortally his yearning to play natural hockey players on artificial ice, rather than vice versa. Jerry likes to project himself as the simple barefoot boy—on skates; but who of us can forget the photograph that Jerry got taken of himself by a very competent photographer, testing out back-hill beaver ponds for November ice thick enough for his skaters to practice on? After this picture was widely published, Jerry's artificial ice was inevitable.

Surely all of us, in anticipation of this dinner, have been reminiscing about what Jerry has meant to us and to Dartmouth. When we arrived in 1926, Jerry was not the youngest of us; but he was not the oldest. When he was born in 1905, our dean, J. Walker Wiggin, was in knee pants. Jerry had more education than most of us, at Somerville High School, at Westbrook Seminary, and at Hebron Academy, and that is probably why he was the sage of Wheeler Hall, a renowned center of liberal learning. Among the elite of us who were the waiters in Freshman Commons, Jerry was not the laziest. John Cheney has laid an all-time claim to that encomium. Jerry was an Eccy major. He reserved his major intellectual enthusiasm, however, for Biblical History. He was a joy to the late "Bib" Woods whose stellar scholar Jerry was. I hope in his later remarks Jerry will give us a few reflections on Biblical History.

As everybody knows, Jerry is *Mr. Dartmouth Hockey.* There are no possible contestants to that title. Last week I asked the Alumni Records Office for a peek at his folder. It is probably the fattest folder in the Class of 1930, with the possible exception of that of

*Ralph Manuel succeeded Mr. Dickerson as Dean of Freshmen in 1972.

the Governor of New York. In the front of it is a fine piece which Charlie Widmayer published in the *Alumni Magazine* in April 1961, written by Jerry's rival coach, Dick Vaughan of Princeton. In this, Vaughan saluted Jerry not merely as Mr. Dartmouth Hockey but as *Mr. College Hockey*. This folder is full of clippings and pictures of Jerry receiving cups, plaques and tributes of all kinds as Coach of the Year, etc., etc., etc.

For us here tonight, all of these things are important. But even more important to us is what you, Jerry, have meant to us. What this is, is hard to put into words. Words that come to mind are: humor, ebullience, impertinence, wisdom, and a great heart. You are a good man with words: an economical man. Four words which you have made unforgettable to Dartmouth hockey players over three decades, words you have painted in large letters on a sign which stands behind the goal at your practice sessions, are: LOOK UP—KEEP FIGHTING.

In our 25th reunion report, the Jeremiah note quotes you as reporting that you have a "Special 4H Club": the first H is for Paul Harmon '13, who first talked to you about coming to Dartmouth; the second H is for Hockey; the third H is for Hanover; and the fourth H is for Happiness. Few of us knew Paul Harmon, so that will be a special, private H for you; there may be a few hockey buffs here who follow the triumphant Bruins, but for most of us *Hockey* begins and ends with Jeremiah; *Hanover* is a joy we all share; *Happiness* is something which you have a rare gift of communicating to your friends and ex-friends alike. For all of us, Jeremiah, Hockey, Hanover, and Happiness are all inextricably intertwined . . .

Jerry, and friends, who of us could think of any four words that we could better say tonight, to ourselves and to each other, than Jerry's famous quadrivium: LOOK UP—KEEP FIGHTING.

Letters

March 15, 1962

Dear Bernie:*

Although I've been very slow in thanking you, I do want to tell you belatedly how much I appreciated your condolences with regard to my recent OPERATION.

I wasn't trying to keep it a secret, heaven knows. The thing is, I've learned, that there isn't any operative procedure in the world that bores people quite so much as a hernia repair. I am nursing the ambition, before too long and before the memory dims, to contribute to society and to hernia-sufferers at least a modest epic on the subject. I note that Rose Kennedy has had one in the last few days and this may contribute something to the status of this procedure. But if it could only have been Jackie . . .

I "went in"—as we heroes of the operating theater like to say—while Herb Williams was still making his brave up-and-down struggle. As you know, Bob Storandt had to get out periodical mimeographed letters to reassure the apprehensive public, and even so, in spite of Bob's best efforts, the stock market went into a prolonged decline.

In this setting, I could hardly ask my friends to toll the bells or ring the tocsin for poor old Dickerson and his hernia repair. This is what makes me especially grateful for your sympathetic note.

Why, in reading the mail—which I was allowed to do on my Good Days—I would find my associates saying: "I am answering your letter of the *blank* inst., since Mr. Dickerson is out of the office briefly for a minor operation . . ."

*Bernard P. Ireland.

Minor! Can you beat that? You can see what my problem was. I won't tell you about my Operation now, but just you wait until I see you next.

Meanwhile, Bernie, my deepest gratitude to you for your sympathy.

Yours faithfully,
A<small>L</small> D<small>ICKERSON</small>

April 4, 1968

Dear Fred:

I was glad to see you stop that lady* who ignored the STOP sign by Thayer Hall last Friday afternoon. I happened to be driving right behind her. If you should detect this subject in any future violations, I hope that you will deal with the matter more sternly. I have tried to do so on numerous occasions, without notable success.

Sincerely,
A. I. DICKERSON

Lt. Fred E. Spencer, Jr.
Campus Police
Box 593

*Mr. Dickerson's wife, Lucia.

This letter was read at a party given for President Dickey on the 24th anniversary of his presidency, and a few months before his retirement.

November 10, 1969

President John Sloan Dickey
Dartmouth College
Hanover, New Hampshire

Dear John:

I'm sorry that, owing to what are known in the trade as "long-standing commitments elsewhere," I cannot join you and our friends tonight in celebration of the event of two dozen years ago, while concurrently saluting a not unrelated event of 62 years ago last Tuesday (which at the time probably did not greatly shake the citizenry of Lock Haven outside the Dickey household).

Our host of this evening (I say "our" host because, although he never actually got around to inviting me, I take his word that he intended to) has suggested that I might contribute a message to the occasion in my capacity, as he put it, of being "the oldest member of the Dartmouth administration." I'm not quite entitled to that designation because I yield 76 days to our still current boss. But our Treasurer has a penchant for flattery and hyperbole. In September, after another distinguished barrister (the one from Seattle) paid his compliments to Dartmouth's last two presidents and some of their associates, John Meck visited my office, nudged me in the gut with a twinkle in his eye, and said: "I've come down to feel your flab."

Anyway, whatever may be the facts about longevity on the Dartmouth payroll, I think it's probably true that I've spent as much time leaning on that windowsill in the President's office as anybody, with the possible exception of Dona Strauss.

These have been 24 wonderfully productive years for Dartmouth; and, although everything hasn't always been roses, these years have included an awful lot of fun for those of us who, while leaning on that windowsill, sitting around conference tables, riding in airplanes and in Voxes 1, 2, 3, 4, 5 and 6, and while sniffing the outdoor air you love so much, have enjoyed your penetrating and frequently mordant analyses of happenings and people, have chuckled at your especially vivid and succinct humor, and have shared, if you will pardon the expression, your wisdom—a wisdom which is characteristically economical with words and determinedly—and, indeed, I'm sure, instinctively—unpompous and thus always fun to share.

I am personally grateful to you for many things which I shall not embarrass you, or bore our friends—who all have their own long lists—by trying to enumerate here. I'll just say that the thing I'm perhaps most grateful for is your staunch insistence, as a sometime traveling companion, that Dickerson does not snore. There are those present, including our host, who would slanderously insist that this is the only blot on your otherwise perfect record of never having uttered a dishonest word.

Having mentioned honesty in a frivolous context, let me seriously say *in absentia* something which would probably seem inappropriate were I present in what I picture as a light-hearted assembly tonight: namely, that among the Dickey qualities this is the one I believe I admire most of all.

You are one not much given to self-congratulation; but as you move about the Dartmouth scene these days, seeing what is visible and tangible and sensing what is invisible but nevertheless palpable (the iceberg metaphor is in order here), I believe that even you cannot help having a good feeling inside about what these 24 years have meant to Dartmouth.

I trust that our host, in spite of the prevailing atmosphere of fiscal austerity, has provided champagne for this occasion. If so, I ask him to raise a glass for me in personal salute to you, John Dickey, and in celebration of what I, who have been here since Eleazar, see as the most productive 24 years in Dartmouth's first two hundred.

Sincerely,
ALBERT I. DICKERSON

P.S.   I am in Boston to be a panelist on the topic: "What Do You Do Now, Dean?" If you have suggestions, the telephone number is 536-5700.

September 8, 1970

Mr. James L. Farley '42
302 Crosby Hall

Dear Jim:

On or about 2:30 p.m. on or about August 27, while I was clipping the edges of our 200 square foot "lawn" at Surfside,* Lucia walked in from our mailbox out on Nonantum Avenue and handed me an envelope which turned out to contain a handwritten note from the President of the College. This exceedingly nice, warm note pointed out that it had come to his attention that on September 1 I would be completing forty years of service to the College. I was not only greatly pleased by this personal attention but also astonished because it had never occurred to me that September 1, 1970, was any special kind of anniversary for me.

Monday night, August 31, was a lovely, stormy night at Surfside and the wind and the waves were making so much noise that it is surprising that we could hear the phone ring; but about 9:00 p.m. it did ring and we did hear it and it turned out to be Harvey Hood, calling from his house in Manchester, Massachusetts (where the surf is a lot quieter) to felicitate me on this anniversary. I have a longstanding, deep affection for Harvey. We had a lovely chat about old times together.

After he hung up I began, inevitably, wondering.

When I got back to Hanover yesterday (Labor Day) and went

*Location of the Dickerson summer cottage on Nantucket Island.

into the office to examine my desk, I found on top of my pile the September 3 issue of the *Valley News,* folded to page 12, and planted on top of that handsome photograph, at the top of column six and seven a bouquet of flowers which I later discovered were the handiwork of our old friend, Kay Brock.

As I read the text, I recognized the style of an old friend and suspected that Farley had been at it again.

Then in due course, in going through the pile of releases from the Office of Information Services, I found the one that had at the bottom "8/28/70 jf."

Mr. Kemeny in his note observed that I had been working for Dartmouth under three presidencies and for "one fifth of the history of the College." This I found a staggering fraction.

In sending my thanks to JGK I pointed out that I had actually started working part-time in the President's Office in April or May of my senior year. I asked him: "What does this do to your fraction?"

Naturally, I expected this to cause JGK to turn to his left, punch a few keys on his computer machine and send me a note saying that yes, indeed, I had served this institution for 20.0007277 per cent of its history.

Actually, this didn't happen.

I keep wondering what in the world led you to doing this piece on my 40th (more or less) anniversary, which in turn leaves me wondering what was the occasion of that long-ago Farleyesque piece on AID and in what medium it appeared? I remember it with pleasure (except for your attributing to me a middle western accent) but I don't seem to have it in my collection.

I'm sure I've told you, as one who has had a sort of lifetime hankering after your profession, that one spring vacation in my senior year I went to New York, armed with letters from Chattanooga friends and spent a wonderful hour with Adolph Ochs in his penthouse office on top of the old *New York Times* building. He said sure, he'd give me a job, but went on with the observation that you and I know so well that he didn't think that the *New York Times* was really the best place for a young journalist to learn the newspaper business. Then I got back to Hanover, soon after Gene Clark's sudden death from pneumonia. Gene was, as you know, Sid Hayward's predecessor as Secretary of the College. Sid and Bob Strong took me out to lunch and offered me a job in the President's Office. You, as a one-time member of the staff of *The Dartmouth*, can understand my astonishment . . .

Anyway, Jim, thanks.

Yours,
AL